THE VOIC

MW00947259

WALKING IN *OVERCOMING POWER* IS THE ONLY WAY
TO OVERCOME STRONGHOLDS, ADDICTIONS, SIN, FLESH
AND THE DEVIL. COUNSELING BY ITSELF DOES NOT
WORK!

THERAPY BY ITSELF DOES NOT WORK!

PSYCHOLOGY BY ITSELF DOES NOT WORK!

STRONGHOLDS ARE NOT MENTAL PROBLEMS.

STRONGHOLDS ARE NOT PHYSICAL PROBLEMS.

STRONGHOLDS ARE SPIRITUAL PROBLEMS, AND MUST BE

DEALT WITH ACCORDING TO THE SPIRITUAL

INSTRUCTION GIVEN TO US BY GOD!

WE ALL HAVE A PAST THAT WE CAN'T CHANGE.

HOWEVER WE DO HAVE A FUTURE THAT WE CAN CHANGE.

EQUIPPING THE BELIEVER IN TODAY'S WORLD.

WATCHMAN RON

HAIMA HOUSE MINISTRIES, INC.

TABLE OF CONTENTS

Title   **Page No.**

Document # 1.. 11
Document # 2.. 21
Document # 3.. 28
Document # 4.. 39
Document # 5.. 50
Document # 6.. 63
Document # 7.. 78
Document # 8.. 92
Document # 9.. 100
Document # 10... 112

Overcoming the Powers of Darkness.............................. 116

Strongholds of:
Addiction 121
Anger 122
Anxiety 123
Bitterness 124
Chaldeans (Witchcraft) 125
Condemnation 126
Confusion 127
Covetousness 128
Criticism 129
Depression 130
Discouragement 131
Disease 132
Disobedience 133
Distress 134
Doubt 135
Fear 136
Greed 137
Guilt 138
Heartache 139
Impatience 140
Inferiority 141
Insecurity 142
Judgment 143
Lying 144
Low Self Esteem 145
Materialism 146
Mistrust.. 147
Negativeness 148
Obesity 149
Oppression 150
Past Hurts 151
Power 152
Poverty 153
Pride 154

Problems 155
Rebellion 156
Rejection 157
Religion 158
Revenge 159
Selfishness 160
Self-Pity 161
Shame 162
Sickness 163
Sin 164
Sorrow 165
Spirit of Heaviness 166
Stress 167
Strife 168
Temptation 169
Thievery 170
Thought 171
Timidity 172
Unbelief 173
Forgiveness 174
Unrighteousness 175
Violence 176
Weakness 177
Worry 178

FORWARD

I would like to recommend my good friends in the ministry, Ron and Carol Grant. I have personally known Ron and Carol for over 20 years. They have faithfully served the Lord and are excellent teachers of the Word of God with signs following.

Ron and Carol have a word in season for today's Church. Many born-again Christians are bound by strongholds of the flesh and the enemy. Ron and Carol teach, step by step, the Church through the Word of God that freedom from strongholds is attainable.

From how to recognize you have a stronghold, to discern the voice of the enemy from our own mind and how to walk in your daily life free from sin, flesh and the devil.

Their ministry is a time-tested, well-rounded gift to the Church. Believers need this spiritual knowledge along with God's power to enable them to stand against the power of evil in these last days.

Their ministry will be a blessing to you and your loved ones. They are humble and caring servants of the Lord Jesus Christ.

I recommend Ron and Carol Grant to the body of Christ without reservation.

Faithfully Yours,

Joan Hunter,

Joan Hunter Ministries

PREFACE

First and above all, I want to give the Lord Jesus all of the Glory for the knowledge that is contained within the pages of this manual. For herein are the "Keys to Freedom" that God, through the power of the Holy Spirit, so graciously opened to me during a period of prayer on a beach in southern England.

I feel very humbled by the knowledge within. Being a Watchman and Pastor of a church, I was led to always pray at length. When I left Bible school, prior to coming to England as a missionary, I had asked my Pastor at the time what to do if I didn't know what to do. My Pastor told me to "just to pray in the Holy Ghost." Well I didn't know what to do, so I began a prayer life of praying three hours every day.

As I began to pray, I began to realize how the Spirit of God was purging me of the old man. The old man that I thought died, "by faith." I had a spirit of lust, prior to being born again, that I would never allow, by an act of my will, to manifest in my marriage, because I loved my wife more than I loved myself, nor did I want to sin against her, or my Lord. I love them both dearly.

However, I could not stop the thoughts, the temptations, or what Paul the Apostle calls, "Fiery Darts." The thoughts would harass me day and night, at times.

What amazed me was the fact that I was praying, reading the word of God, even ministering the word of God, and still I could not get the thoughts, *fiery darts*, and the temptations to stop. *Thoughts from the past, thoughts of lust, even came while I was in prayer.*

I began to get desperate and cry out to God. I saw a known evangelist fall to sexual addiction. I knew God would help me.

I then made up my mind that I was going to get an answer from God. I went daily to a beach in southern England, and stayed in prayer until I got an answer from God.

During those months of prayer, God began to reveal the "VOICE OF HIS BLOOD".

I began to notice after a few days of prayer that there seemed to be a divine order to what the Lord was showing me.

As I placed all the different scriptures and text together in the order that I received them, I began to realize that God had given me answers to questions some of us have had. *Why am I born again and bound? Resurrected and not yet released?*

God was revealing to me spiritual knowledge on how to overcome sin, flesh, and the devil. How to overcome thoughts and SPIRITUAL harassment. How to overcome temptations of the flesh. How to overcome sin. How to overcome ANY onslaught of the enemy.

God was revealing the enemy of my soul.

The opening of the eyes of our understanding and Spiritual knowledge of the truth of God's Word is absolutely necessary for deliverance from the spirit of deception.

Without the opening of the eyes of our Spiritual understanding, freedom is impossible. Satan can actually overcome us and bring us into bondage even when we believe God by faith, if we do not exert action in the Spiritual realm. When you have discerned the deception of the enemy, and recognize the conversations of the enemy within the mind and wills of the flesh, (that of physical impulse) you will begin to gain ground on the enemy of your soul.

Deception unlatches the gate for evil spirits to come in; passivity provides a place for them to stay. This combination of deception and passivity equals entrenchment of the soul, (mind, will, emotions). The common factor for entrenchment is the inactivity of your own God given free will.

We as Christians in our ignorance have been deceived by the powers of the darkness and have fulfilled the conditions for the enemy to work in our lives.

There are four steps the enemy lays down to trap us.

1. Ignorance – A lack of spiritual knowledge, education, or being unaware of the enemy at work in our lives.
2. Deception – A deliberate act by the enemy to deprive us of our God given freedom paid for in full by the Blood of Jesus Christ.
3. Passivity – Inactivity on our behalf exerting no resistance in the spiritual realm against the enemy of our soul.
4. Entrenchment – The enemy has fortified his stronghold and taken the Christian captive by the combination of ignorance, deception, and our own passivity.

You will learn how to overcome entrenchment of the soul if you will follow the instructions given by God contained within the pages of this book.

Entrenchment is the stronghold that is causing you to do the things that are contrary to the Word of God. When you have a situation in your life that is controlling you and you are not able to stop or overcome it in the natural, you are entrenched by the enemy of your soul.

This entrenchment can also be an addition. An example would be those that are caught up in pornography. This addiction actually causes the brain to release endogenous chemicals. Endogenous means, "produced from within". Cocaine or alcohol seek to mimic the brain's natural chemicals, pornography releases the real thing within the body. This is today's new addiction.

It does not matter the depth of the entrenchment, as long as you decide daily to choose the will of God in your life and do it.

This attitude will give God the opportunity to work His will in your and cause the influence of strongholds and wills of the flesh at work to weaken which in turn will strengthen you spiritually. We must allow the Holy Spirit to rule over our renewed mind, will, and emotions. When we as children of God allow the flesh to rule, we will be rebellious to the things of God. When the Holy Spirit is allowed to rule, we produce spiritual fruit and the power of self-control.

Proverbs 25:28 – He that hath no rule over his own spirit is like a city that is broken down and without walls.

Let us go on to perfection!

The spiritual knowledge found in this manual not only set me free, it will set any born again Christian free of ANY STRONGHOLD OR ADDICTION that may be resident in their soul, and who follows these directions given from the very hand of God to His children...

WATCHMAN RON

THIS GUIDEBOOK IS LOVINGLY DEDICATED

TO MY BELOVED AND DEVOTED WIFE,

CAROL

FAITHFUL COMPANION IN THE MINISTRY OF

THE WORD

AND TRULY A GIFT TO ME FROM GOD

I WANT TO ALSO GIVE HONORABLE MENTION OF MY

BROTHER IN CHRIST AN INTREGAL PART OF THIS MINISTRY

ROBERT A. FARMER

A FAITHFUL ASSOCIATE

THE VOICE OF HIS BLOOD

STRESSING THE LIMITATIONS OF MAN

The word "HAIMA" is the Greek word in the Bible for BLOOD. It stresses the limitations of humanity.

We have been set free, healed, and delivered by the BLOOD of JESUS.

We have been BORN AGAIN by the BLOOD, saved from eternal death and separation from God. (John 3:3)

We have been REDEEMED by the BLOOD, bought back from the power of sin and death. (Eph. 1:7)

We have received ATONEMENT by the BLOOD, the act by which God restores a relationship of harmony and unity between Himself and human beings. (Rom. 5:11)

We have been made RIGHTEOUS by the BLOOD. God transfers the righteousness of JESUS to those who trust in Him. (2 Cor. 5:21)

We are SANCTIFIED by the BLOOD. The process of God's grace by which we are separated from sin. (Heb. 10:10)

We are JUSTIFIED by the BLOOD. God charges the sin of man to JESUS and credits the righteousness of JESUS to the believer. (Rom. 5:9)

We are RECONCILED by the BLOOD. The initiative was taken by God while we were still sinners and enemies; God has reconciled us to Himself. (Rom. 5:10)

We are FORGIVEN by the BLOOD. God has pardoned the sin of human beings. (Col. 2: 13-14)

We have been DELIVERED by the BLOOD. The act of being delivered from the power of darkness, set at liberty from captivity. (Col. 1:13)

We have received OVERCOMING POWER by the BLOOD. The power we receive when we act upon what has been delegated to us.

WE HAVE BEEN:

BORN AGAIN BY THE BLOOD

REDEEMED BY THE BLOOD

RECEIVED ATONEMENT BY THE BLOOD

MADE RIGHTEOUS BY THE BLOOD

SANCTIFIED BY THE BLOOD

JUSTIFIED BY THE BLOOD

RECONCILED BY THE BLOOD

FORGIVEN BY THE BLOOD

DELIVERED BY THE BLOOD

RECEIVED OVERCOMING POWER BY THE BLOOD

BY THE BLOOD, BY THE BLOOD, BY THE BLOOD

WHAT IS THE PROBLEM?

WHY ARE YOU STILL BOUND ?

BORN AGAIN AND BOUND?

RESURRECTED AND NOT YET RELEASED?

PRISONERS IN THE PROMISED LAND?

YOU ARE NOT WALKING IN THE OVERCOMING POWER THAT HAS BEEN GIVEN TO YOU BY THE BLOOD.

Luke 10:19

Behold, I give unto you power to tread on serpents and scorpions and over all the power of the enemy: and nothing shall by any means hurt you.

Rev 12:11

And they overcame him by the blood of the Lamb and by the word of their testimony; and they loved not their lives unto the death.

Eph. 2:6

And hath raised us up together, and made us sit together in heavenly places in Christ Jesus.

WALKING IN OVERCOMING POWER IS THE ONLY WAY TO OVERCOME ADDICTIONS!

WALKING IN OVERCOMING POWER IS THE ONLY WAY TO OVERCOME SIN, FLESH AND THE DEVIL.

COUNSELING BY ITSELF DOES NOT WORK!

THERAPY BY ITSELF DOES NOT WORK!

PSYCHOLOGY BY ITSELF DOES NOT WORK!

STRONGHOLDS ARE NOT MENTAL PROBLEMS.

STRONGHOLDS ARE NOT PHYSICAL PROBLEMS.

STRONGHOLDS ARE SPIRITUAL PROBLEMS AND MUST BE DEALT WITH ACCORDING TO THE SPIRITUAL INSTRUCTION GIVEN TO US BY GOD!

I HAVE BEEN WHERE YOU ARE AT.

I CRIED OUT TO GOD ON A BEACH IN SOUTHERN ENGLAND FOR ANSWERS.

GOD HEARD MY PRAYERS, GOD HEARD MY INTERCESSION, AND GOD HEARD MY CRIES!

GOD REVEALED THE ANSWERS TO MY PRAYERS.

HOW TO OVERCOME AN ENEMY WHO IS DECEIVING GOD'S PEOPLE.

Matt 16:17

And Jesus answered and said unto him, Blessed art thou, Simon Barjona: for flesh and blood hath not revealed it unto thee, but my Father, which is in heaven.

I HAVE BEEN BLESSED TO RECEIVE THIS REVELATION KNOWLEDGE.

I HAVE BEEN BLESSED TO RECEIVE THIS SPIRITUAL KNOWLEDGE.

GOD WANTS TO BLESS YOU NOW THROUGH THE VOICE OF HIS BLOOD

THIS GUIDE BOOK EXPLAINS THE SPIRITUAL WEAPONS GOD HAS GIVEN TO HIS CHILDREN AND ALSO HOW TO USE THIS SPIRITUAL POWER TO OVERCOME SIN, FLESH, AND THE DEVIL.

John 8:32

And ye shall know the truth, and the truth shall make you free.

WATCHMAN RON

HAIMA HOUSE MINISTRIES, INC.

PAUL THE APOSTLE TELLS US IN GAL 3:3

Gal. 3:3

Are ye so foolish? Having begun in the Spirit, are ye now made perfect by the flesh?

What we are seeing in the church of today is not the fruit of perfection, not the maturing of the saints, in their daily walk as Christians.

Many are born again and bound, resurrected and not yet released, prisoners in the Promised Land.

Many are bound by strongholds of the enemy and don't realize it, or believe God for their deliverance by "faith" when the price has already been paid for in full at the cross.

This manual is based on the Word of God and my personal experience as a Pastor who has been through this experience, not only with his congregation, but also with himself. Let us go on to perfection!

Every born again child of God that I have ever met has the desire to become the overcomer the Bible talks about.

To overcome behavior problems of the old man, the old self-life. The Bible tells us in Hosea 4:6, "my people are destroyed for lack of knowledge."

This knowledge is SPIRITUAL KNOWLEDGE. **For without** SPIRITUAL KNOWLEDGE, **we are vulnerable to the enemy of our soul.**

Col. 1:9

For this cause, we also, since the day we heard it, do not cease to pray for you, and to desire that ye might be filled with the knowledge of his will in all wisdom and spiritual understanding…

We must overcome sin, flesh, and the devil!

We overcome by yielding to the will of God!

We read in Matt. 6:10, "Thy Kingdom come, thy will be done, in earth as it is in heaven.

Jesus, who is our example in all things says to our Father in Luke 22:42 "nevertheless not my will, but thine be done". Can we do any less for our heavenly Father?

The battle of the wills, (whom we are going to serve), between our flesh and our spirit-man is a daily battle, and to be an overcomer, this battle must be won in the mind.

The enemy uses the mind for a battleground. Our flesh consists of three parts: MIND, WILL, EMOTION--EACH HAS IT'S OWN WILL!

We must always remember this, as the enemy will use one or all of these to ascend over us and take us captive in the process!

When God created us, He gave us a free will to choose daily to overcome sin, flesh, and the devil!

God gave His church and the believer authority on this earth to be an overcomer of sin, flesh, and the devil.

The knowledge in this MANUAL, when used properly will help you to overcome any stronghold that may be in your life.

IT IS IMPERATIVE THAT YOU READ EVERY WORD OF GOD IN THIS BOOK. THE HOLY SPIRIT WILL OPEN YOUR UNDERSTANDING TO THE SPIRITUAL REALM, AND WHAT YOU ARE DEALING WITH IN REGARDS TO STRONGHOLDS THAT MAY BE RESIDENT IN YOUR SOUL.

A LETTER TO THE CHURCH OF CHRIST FROM PAUL THE APOSTLE:

Eph. 1:17-19

17   That the God of our Lord Jesus Christ, the Father of glory, may give unto you the spirit of wisdom and revelation in the knowledge of him:

18   That the eyes of your understanding being enlightened; that ye may know what is the hope of his calling, and what the riches of the glory of his inheritance in the saints,

19   And what is the exceeding greatness of his Power to us-ward who believe, according to working of his mighty power

Why is Paul the apostle praying that we have the *eyes of our understanding enlightened*?
That we may receive the Spirit of wisdom and revelation and know what is the hope of God's calling and the greatness of HIS POWER given to us!
Because the eyes of our understanding have been blinded by darkness.
We have been deceived by darkness about the power given to us.

Eph. 4:18

Having the understanding darkened, **being alienated from the life of God through the ignorance that is in them,** because of the blindness of their heart:
What understanding?
Spiritual Understanding and about Spiritual Power!

Col. 1:9

For this cause we also, since the day we heard it, do not cease to pray for you, and to desire that ye might be filled with the knowledge of his will in all wisdom and spiritual understanding;
Matt 15:16
And Jesus said, are ye also yet without understanding?
We must have spiritual understanding to understand the mysteries of God.
THE SOURCE OF STRONGHOLDS, THE WILLS OF THE FLESH, AND HOW THEY OPERATE WITHIN THE SOUL OF THE BELIEVER.

Cor. 10:3-5

3   For though we walk in the flesh, we do not war after the flesh:

4   (For the weapons of our warfare are not carnal, but mighty through God to the pulling down of strongholds;)

5   Casting down imaginations, and every high thing that exalteth itself against the knowledge of God, and bringing into captivity every thought to the obedience of Christ;

What are these strongholds the word of God is speaking of?
A stronghold sets in the center of a fortification surrounded by two walls.
Around the stronghold is a wall that's called, *"arguments, theories, and reasoning"*.
(Thoughts from the enemy's camp.)
Around the first wall is a second wall that's called, *"high and lofty things"*. (Pride)
Both of these fortified walls must come down.
In the center of the fortification is the root of the stronghold that was placed there by the enemy of your soul.

The Voice of HIS Blood teachs you how to recognize and tear down these strongholds.

Rom. 11:16
If the root be holy, so are the branches.
Because we are created in the image of God, we are made up of three parts: SPIRIT...SOUL...BODY
God is Spirit, and created us.
Which was created first? ...SPIRIT, SOUL, OR BODY?

SPIRIT !

For the Spirit of God created our soul and body.
As a born again Christian, our spirit is born again instantly, set free from the power of sin and death, and brought into right standing with God. (Rom. 8:2)
We are new creatures through Christ Jesus. (2 Corin. 5:17)
Our soul and body are not born again.
This is why we are told in God's word to renew our minds to the word of God. (Rom. 12:2)
We live in our body and will be redeemed at the Rapture, either alive or from the grave. (1 Thess. 4:15-17)
Our body is the physical container for our spirit and soul (2 Peter 1: 13-14)
The Bible calls it our tabernacle, our temple, a clay pot.

2 Corin. 10:3-5
5 ...INASMUCH AS WE REFUTE ARGUMENTS AND THEORIES AND REASONING. (AMP)

Arguments, Theories and Reasoning **come from the mind and are the first wall of fortification.**

These *arguments, theories, reasoning* **come from the mind, not from the spirit or the body.**

WHY? Because ...Our spirit man is born again!
Our body is our container, or vessel.
Our soul is our personality, and is also made up of three parts:

> **MIND...WILL...EMOTIONS**
> **MIND...HOW WE THINK,**
> **WILL...HOW WE BEHAVE,**
> **EMOTIONS... HOW WE FEEL.**

All sin originates in the mind in the form of a thought, fiery dart, or a temptation.
This is why the mind is the battleground.
It is important to understand this as the Bible teaches us that the Spirit of God inhabits us, and the Spirit does not produce sin.
We are partakers of our Fathers divine nature. (2 Peter 1:4)
Yet the Bible makes it clear that a Christian can sin. (Romans 7:23)
God has given us a free will to choose daily whom we will serve.

Romans 7:23

But I discern in my bodily members (in the sensitive appetites and wills of the flesh) a different law (rule of action) at war against the law of my mind (my reasoning) and making me prisoner to the law of sin that dwells in my bodily organs (in the sensitive appetites and wills of the flesh.) (AMP)

We have sensitive appetites and wills of the flesh at war with our mind.

Sin does not originate in the believer's spirit. (2 Peter 1:4)

Sin originates in the mind in the form of a temptation, a thought, or a fiery dart.

It is the flesh that sins, not your spirit.

Paul the Apostle is speaking in Romans 7:23 of the sin nature and wills of the flesh.

What are wills of the Flesh?

Example: OBESITY

Have you ever seen an overweight, Jewish person in the concentration camps of Nazi Germany during WW II?

The Jewish people were dominated by the Gestapo who over rode their will not allowing them to eat.

This is a picture of how Satan operates.

The Gestapo overrode their will, took them captive, and made slaves out of them.

Satan wants to override our will and take us captive making us slaves to sin.

Satan wants to override our will using strongholds of the mind and wills of the flesh.

Prior to being born again Satan did control us through the sin nature.

However, as a born again Christian, Satan cannot legally do so because we have been delivered from the power of sin and death. (Rom. 8:2)

Also, our old man died with Jesus on the cross. (Rom. 6:6)

We must give the enemy ground by an act of our own free will.

Satan will use strongholds from our past, prior to being born again, to tempt our flesh to sin.

Gal 3:3

Are ye so foolish? Having begun in the Spirit, are ye now made perfect by the flesh?

The Flesh has its own will.

This is why people have addictions.

Addictions are located in the flesh.

Is a stronghold an evil spirit? NO!

A stronghold is the vehicle used by evil spirits to tempt our flesh, which in turn triggers an addiction, if we allow it to do so.

We still must act upon the temptation, by an act of our own free will

WE HAVE A FREE WILL.

Strongholds are the habits, behavior, and thought patterns that were built up within our mind while we were still servants of sin.

These habits, behavior and thought patterns leave us exposed to the enemy's influence and deception.

Addictions of the flesh are a result of these existing strongholds.

Although we are born again, we still have to overcome the sin nature.

We still have to overcome sinful flesh.

We still have to overcome the old man.

That is why Paul the Apostle calls it... WILLS OF THE FLESH

FLESH IS ADDICTED TO WHAT IT LIKES.

FLESH LIKES WHAT EVER GIVES IT PLEASURE.

Satan knows that if he can tempt our flesh, he has an opportunity to get his hooks in us and to strengthen his strongholds.

Strongholds destroy our opportunity to live the abundant life.
Strongholds make us Prisoners in the Promised Land.
Born Again and Bound...Resurrected and not yet released.
Individual strongholds can differ from person to person, and yet they have certain characteristics that remain constant.
Most people give up and simply learn to live with them.
Some are subdued through medication or drugs or alcohol.

The main characteristics are:

1) **Strongholds are stubborn.**
   If we attack them in our own strength, they will reappear over and over.

2) **Strongholds are uncontrollable.**
   If you have a habit or behavior problem that controls you....you have a stronghold in your life.

3) **Strongholds of a sexual nature are your deepest darkest secret!**
   With God's supernatural weapons, such strongholds are destroyed.
   Most Christians do not realize they have strongholds until the Lord shows them to you.

Before being born again, we were servants of sin.
Let's look at our condition prior to being born again.

Eph. 2:1-3
1   And you hath he quickened, who were dead in trespasses and sins;
2   Wherein in time past ye walked according to the course of this world, according to the prince of the power of the air, the spirit that now worketh in the children of disobedience:
3   Among whom also we all had our conversation in times past in the lusts of our flesh, fulfilling the desires of the flesh and of the mind; and were by nature the children of wrath, even as others.

Most Christians are still having these conversations with the enemy of their soul.
These conversations in times past, in the lusts of our flesh, fulfilling the desires of the flesh and of the mind, are the foundation of strongholds.
What is this conversation in times past?
Remember: A stronghold is the vehicle used by evil spirits to override your free will.
Evil spirits use strongholds of lust within the mind to bring to your remembrance the pleasures, the experiences of past sin, especially sexual sin, to entice you to act upon these thoughts and temptations.
Evil spirits use strongholds of lust within the mind to bring forth fantasies and vain imaginations.
Evil spirits use strongholds to tempt your flesh to sin against a Holy God.
Evil spirits use strongholds of conversation of the old man to get you angry, bitter, or to make you to criticize someone.
Evil spirits use strongholds of conversation to bring discouragement and oppress you.
Evil spirits use conversations to make you fearful, *to paralyze you*.
Evil Spirits use strongholds of conversations to make you greedy or impatient.

Evil spirits use strongholds of conversation to tempt you to tell lies.

Evil spirits use conversations to bring to your remembrance past hurts, rejection, or low self-esteem.

Evil spirits use strongholds of conversation (with self) to bring about self-pity and selfishness.

Evil spirits use strongholds of conversation to tempt you to steal.

Evil spirits use conversations of doubt and unbelief, or worry.

Evil spirits use strongholds of un-forgiveness.

Evil spirits use strongholds of lust, within the mind, to bring to your remembrance the pleasures, the experiences of past sin, especially sexual sin, to keep you addicted.

Evil Spirits use strongholds of lust to entice you into sexual addiction.

These are only a few of the strongholds the enemy is using to destroy our abundant life.

What does the Word of God tell us to do?

Eph. 4:22-27,30

22 that ye put off concerning the former conversation the old man, which is corrupt according to the deceitful lusts

23 And be renewed in the spirit of your mind;

23 and that ye put on the new man, which after God is created in righteousness and true holiness.

25 wherefore putting away lying, speak every man truth with his neighbor: for we are members one of another.

26 Be ye angry, and sin not: let not the sun go down upon your wrath:

27 Neither give place to the devil.

30 And grieve not the Holy Spirit of God, whereby ye are sealed unto the day of redemption.

We are to put off these former conversations of the old man.

We are to be renewed in our mind.

We are to put on the new man.

We are to give no place to the devil.

We are to not grieve the Holy Spirit of God.

Thoughts…Fiery Darts…Evil spirits use strongholds of conversation with our old man.

Why does the Word of God call them *Fiery Darts*?

Because they are able start a raging fire in your flesh if they are not quenched.

A raging fire of the flesh that we want to put out using carnal methods.

We have to use supernatural spiritual power from God to overcome these fiery darts.

God has not left us defenseless against the forces of darkness.

Our weapons have been fashioned and issued by God.

We have supernatural, spiritual weapons capable of withstanding and overcoming principalities, powers, and rulers of darkness

Eph. 6:10-18

10 Finally, my brethren, be strong in the Lord, and in the power of his might. (The Holy Ghost)

11 Put on the whole (all) armor of God, that ye may be able to stand against the wiles (strategies) of the devil.

12 For we wrestle not against flesh and blood, (people) but against principalities, against powers, against the rulers of the darkness of this world, against spiritual wickedness in high places.

13 Wherefore take unto you the whole (all) armor of God that ye may be able to withstand in the evil day, and having done all, to stand.

14 Stand therefore, having your loins girt about with truth, and having on the breastplate of righteousness;

15 and your feet shod with the preparation of the gospel of peace;

16 Above all, taking the shield of faith, wherewith ye shall be able to quench all the fiery darts (thoughts, temptations) of the wicked (one).

17 And take the helmet of salvation, and the sword of the Spirit, (no scabbard) which is the word of God:

18 Praying always with all prayer and supplication in the Spirit, and watching thereunto with all perseverance and supplication for all saints.

Verse 16--FIERY DARTS, THOUGHTS, VAIN IMAGINATIONS = STRONGHOLDS.

These *thoughts, fiery darts, and vain imaginations* are temptations to get our flesh to sin against God.

The battlefield is in the mind.

We are to cast down fiery darts, thoughts, and vain imaginations.
STRONGHOLDS ARE THOUGHTS, FIERY DARTS,
TEMPTATIONS OF: GREED, TEMPER, GUILT, PAST SIN, LUST
OF THE FLESH, DEPRESSION, FEAR OPPRESSION, HURTS
FROM THE PAST, CHILD ABUSE, CONFUSION, SELFISHNESS,
INSECURITY, SELF-CENTEREDNESS, PRIDE,
DISCOURGEMENT, ANGER, RAGE, PORNOGRAPHY, SEXUAL
SIN, SEXUAL BONDAGE, ADULTRY, FORNICATION,
HOMOSEXUALITY, CRITICISM, DOUBT, IMPATIENCE, SEXUAL
PERVERSION, LYING, LOW SELF- ESTEEM, MATERIALISM,
REBELLION, REJECTION, REVENGE, SELF-PITY, STRESS,
STRIFE, THIEVERY, UNBELIEF, VIOLENCE, WORRY...
These, and many other strongholds, come from our past.

Gal 5:16-17

16 This I say then, Walk in the Spirit, and ye shall not fulfil the lust of the flesh.

17 For the flesh lusteth against the Spirit, and the Spirit against the flesh: and these are contrary the one to the other: so that ye cannot do the things that ye would.

2 Cor. 10:5
Casting down imaginations, and every high thing that exalteth itself against the knowledge of God, and bringing into captivity every thought to the obedience of Christ;
John 10:10
The thief cometh not, but for to steal, and to kill, and to destroy: I am come that they might have life, and that they might have it more abundantly.
Strongholds can steal our joy, our peace.
Strongholds destroy relationships.
Strongholds destroy the opportunity for the abundant life.
Strongholds are the main cause of divorce. Strongholds disrupt the family.

Strongholds destroy marriages.
Strongholds keep you captive.
Prisoners in the Promised Land.
Born Again and Still Bound.
Resurrected and not yet released.

WINNING THE BATTLE IS NOT THE DIFFICULT PART!
IT IS RECOGNIZING THE BATTLE.
IT IS RECOGNIZING YOUR WEAPONS.
IT IS RECOGNIZING THE ENEMY.
IT IS RECOGNIZING WHO YOU ARE IN CHRIST JESUS!
IT IS KNOWING HOW TO OVERCOME THE ENEMY!

How did strongholds enter into your life, in the first place?
THOUGHTS, FIERY DARTS, VAIN IMAGINATIONS!
BRICK BY BRICK, ONE AT A TIME, BRICK BY BRICK... THOUGHTS,
FIERY DARTS, AND VAIN IMAGINATIONS.
This battle to overcome the enemy's stronghold is a Spiritual battle. This is the
reason we have Sspiritual weapons.
When we have completely won this battle, the victory WILL drop into YOUR heart.
You have won.
Now the prize of overcoming whatever stronghold you have had is yours.
You have your reward.
The strongest battle, in the beginning, is to recognize you must fight to overcome the
stronghold.
You must realize God is with us.
GOD wants us to overcome.
Our weapons have been fashioned and issued.
These supernatural Spiritual weapons are more than capable of overcoming
principalities, powers, and rulers of darkness.

2 Cor. 10:4
For the weapons of our warfare are not carnal, but mighty through God to the
pulling down of strong holds.

WHAT DO YOU HAVE TO DO TO OVERCOME THESE STRONGHOLDS OF
THE ENEMY?
WHAT DO YOU HAVE TO DO TO OVERCOME ADDICTIONS THAT ARE IN
YOUR FLESH?

Eph. 6:11
Put on the whole (ALL OF IT) armor of God, that ye may be able to stand against
the wiles (STRATEGIES) of the devil.
WHY?

Eph. 6:16
...ye shall be able to (QUENCH) all the fiery darts (THOUGHTS)
(TEMPTATIONS) of the wicked (one).
You must have the revelation that you can overcome.
Believing we can overcome is the first phase of the battle.

Fight every thought of defeat from the enemy.
Satan wants to stop you before you start.
Strongholds come from the "old man", what we were before we were born again.

When we are born again, we are new creatures, "new men", through Christ Jesus. We are a three part being: spirit, soul, body.

Our spirit is born again, our body we live in, but our soul is neither of these.

Our soul also has three parts: mind, will, emotions. *This is where the battle is.*

Satan is using strongholds to overcome you, through thoughts of the mind and temptations of the flesh.

Satan does this to capture our free will to get us to sin against a Holy God, by an act of our own free will.

Those suffering from this problem have to be taught how to overcome these thoughts and temptations.
This is a spiritual battle that will have to be won. Strongholds do not go away by themselves they must be overcome.

Example:
Sexual Addiction is a stronghold that is in the flesh, and because of its sensual pleasure, those addicted keep returning to it when they are tempted.

This addiction does not just go away all by itself. It will stay with you until you, by an act of your own free will, decide to overcome it, according to the Spiritual instructions God has given to us through His Word regarding how to overcome. There is no other way.

In our experience, counseling by itself does not work.

God has made a way but we must understand how to overcome Spiritually.

THE VOICE OF HIS BLOOD, *teaches you how to overcome, and also shows you how to overcome.*

God has made this ministry available so that you will be able to learn how to overcome the Strongholds that the enemy has placed in your life, and the life of your loved ones.

Thank you Jesus.

John 10:10
The thief cometh not, but for to steal, and to kill, and to destroy: I am come that they might have life, and that they might have it more abundantly.

Men of God, you are the Priest in the home. You have the authority to go after the thief.
Jesus said in Luke 17:21, "The Kingdom of God is within you…" …KINGDOM AUTHORITY…

John 19:2
And the soldiers platted a crown of thorns, and put it on his head, and they put on him a purple robe…

The Roman soldiers placed a crown of thorns upon the head of Jesus on the way to the cross.
A crown represents authority.
The thorns represent the fiery darts that were piercing the head of Jesus where the mind is located.
Jesus shed His blood for our sin.
Jesus shed His blood for our healing.
Jesus also shed His blood for our total freedom.
He gave us authority over fiery darts of the enemy.
We have been set free, healed, and delivered at the cross, by the precious Blood of the lamb. By the BLOOD! By the BLOOD!

FATHER:
I DECLARE THAT:
I WILL OBEY GOD'S WILL.
I WILL RESIST SATAN'S WILL
I WILL EXERCISE MY OWN WILL.
I DECLARE BY AN ACT OF MY FREE WILL THAT:
I CHOOSE FREEDOM.
I WANT LIBERTY.
I REFUSE TO BE PASSIVE.
I WILL SEVER EVERY RELATIONSHIP WITH DARKNESS.
I WILL BE MY OWN MASTER.
I RESOLVE TO CONTROL MYSELF.
I WILL JOIN MY WILL TO GOD'S WILL TO RECOVER ALL LOST GROUND.
THE PAST IS OVER.
THIS IS A DAY OF NEW BEGINNINGS.
THANK YOU FATHER, FOR GIVING ME A FREE WILL TO CHOOSE THIS DAY WHOM I WILL SERVE.
THANK YOU JESUS FOR GOING TO THE CROSS, BY AN ACT OF YOUR OWN FREE WILL, AND SHEDDING YOUR BLOOD FOR ME.
STEP BY STEP WE WILL ASCEND TO TOTAL FREEDOM. THANK YOU JESUS!

Reread and meditate on this document until you fully understand the entire content before moving on to document #2.
If you are having a problem understanding the content, pray and ask the Holy Spirit to enlighten the eyes of your understanding.

WATCHMAN RON

THE POWER OF THE HOLY GHOST
Jesus said in Luke 24:49, "And, behold, I send the promise of my Father upon you: but tarry ye in the city of Jerusalem, until ye be endued with power from on high".
After Jesus was raised from the dead, He appeared to His disciples many times. For the period of forty days, He was with the disciples, teaching them about the Kingdom of God. Yet they still needed something from God before they would be ready to go out with the "Good News".
Our Lord Jesus Christ said that they needed to baptized in the HOLY GHOST!

Acts 1:2-5
2   Until the day in which he was taken up, after that **he through the Holy Ghost,** had given commandments unto the apostles whom he had chosen:
3   To whom also he shewed himself alive after his passion by many infallible proofs, being seen of them forty days, and speaking of the things pertaining to the kingdom of God:
4   And, being assembled together with them, **commanded them** that they should not depart from Jerusalem, **but wait for the promise of the Father**, which, saith he, ye have heard of me
5   For John truly baptized with water; **but ye shall be baptized with the Holy Ghost** not many days hence…

We are commanded to be filled with the Holy Spirit!

Acts 1:8
But ye shall receive power, after that the Holy Ghost is come upon you: **and ye shall be witnesses unto me both in Jerusalem, and in all Judaea, and in Samaria, and unto the uttermost part of the earth.**
My dear people, **we are endued with power.** When we are filled with the Holy Ghost, the Word of God is telling us that we have been given miraculous power, and ability to operate in the supernatural realm.

We overcome through the Holy Ghost… we can do nothing without Him!

The original Greek word for power is: (Strongs concordance) "1411 dunamis (doo'-nam-is); force, miraculous power (usually by implication, a miracle itself): KJV-- ability, abundance, meaning, might (-ily, -y, -y

deed), (worker of) miracle (-s), power, strength, violence, mighty (wonderful) work. And God has given us the freedom of action [authority, by the use of our own free will!] to be overcomers.
Also the Greek word (exousia denotes "freedom of action, right to act"; used of God, it is absolute, unrestricted, used of men, authority is delegated). Angelic beings are called "powers" (Vine's Expository Dictionary of Biblical words).
ON the day of Pentecost (Acts 2:1-4) was the Body of Christ's entrance into the supernatural realm, Glory to God! (We have been given power to overcome!) The baptism of the Holy Ghost manifested itself in a supernatural way! All 120 believers, plus Mary, were filled with the Holy Ghost, and began to speak in other tongues!
The disciples, all 120, plus Mary, now had the same Holy Ghost that indwelt Jesus during His earthly ministry!

They began to fulfill the supernatural ministry that Our Lord Jesus Christ had begun. They were endued with the Power of the Holy Ghost. This was OUR introduction into the supernatural miracle working power, supernatural anointing, supernatural authority, and supernatural ability, of the Holy Ghost!
What do you think the job of the Holy Ghost is? The same as it has always been! To overcome principalities, powers, and rulers of darkness, of this world.

Jesus has told us in the Word of God:
John 14:12
Verily, verily, I say unto you, He that believeth on me, the works that I do shall he do also; and greater works than these shall he do; because I go unto my Father.
Jesus intends for the Body of Christ to walk in that same supernatural power, supernatural authority, supernatural anointing, and supernatural ability of the Holy Ghost! (to be overcomers)
Jesus tells us in John 16:7, "However, I am telling you nothing but the truth when I say it is profitable (good, expedient, advantageous) for you that I go away.
Because if I do not go away, (the Counselor, Helper, Advocate, Intercessor, Strengthener) will not come to you (into close fellowship with you); but if I go away, I will send Him to you (to be in close fellowship with you)."
Jesus said: It is advantageousness for you that He goes away!
Why? So the Comforter (the Holy Ghost) can come, so He can have place in our lives. The Holy Ghost is our Counselor, Helper, Advocate, Intercessor, Strengthener, and Standby. (AMP) (To help us be overcomers)
We have to give the Holy Ghost place in our lives by an act of our own will. We must have the revelation that God will not usurp authority over us. God has given us a free will.
We read in verse 8 of John 16, "And when He comes, He will convict and convince the world and bring demonstration to it about sin and about righteousness".
God will confirm His Word through the Holy Ghost. (Mark 16:20) "And they went forth, and preached everywhere, the Lord working with them, and confirming the word with signs following. Amen
We read in verse 15 of John 16, "Everything that the Father has is Mine. That is what I meant when I said that He (the Spirit) will take the things that are mine and reveal (declare ,disclose, transmit) it to you". (AMP)
The Holy Ghost hears from the Father. The Holy Ghost reveals...**revelation knowledge comes through the Holy Ghost and is transmitted to us.** (If your receiver is turned on!) (An act of our will.)
We need the Spirit of Truth, (The Holy Ghost) to receive and understand mysteries of the Kingdom of God! *The mysteries of the supernatural realm.*
God is Spirit, and the Spiritual realm is what created us, who live in the natural, let me ask you, which is more real? What you see, or what you don't see?
Jesus came to bridge the gap, by taking on flesh, to tell and demonstrate to we believers the Kingdom of God...the Kingdom that created us!
Signs and wonders are performed by the Holy Ghost!
Paul the Apostle tells us in Romans 15:19, "Even as my preaching has been accompanied with the power of signs and wonders, (and all of it) by the power of the Holy Ghost. (AMP)
The Holy Ghost is a gift, a promise, to all of the Body of Christ, not just a select few!

Acts 2:38-39
38 Then Peter said unto them, Repent, and be baptized every one of you in the name

39 of Jesus Christ for the remission of sins, and **ye shall receive the gift of the Holy Ghost**

40 **For the promise is unto you, and to your children**, and to all that are afar off, even as many as the Lord our God shall call.

The Holy Ghost honors and Glorifies Jesus Christ!

John 16:14, "He shall glorify me: for he shall receive of mine, and shall shew it unto you..."

The Holy Ghost is supernatural. He is our supernatural Counselor, our supernatural Helper, our supernatural Advocate, our supernatural Intercessor, our supernatural Strengthener, our supernatural Standby!
We serve a supernatural, Almighty God. Glory to His name!

The Holy Ghost is the One who teaches, trains, and guides us.
It is very important that we become sensitive to the Holy Ghost.

The Holy Ghost is the one who brings the power of God, the Glory of God, into manifestation here on the earth.

The Holy Ghost is supernatural. Now you know why the Lord has told us not to leave home without Him.

The Holy Ghost teaches, trains, and guides us to become overcomers!

The Word of God instructs us in Eph. 6:18, "Pray at all times on every occasion, in every season, in the Spirit." *That's right, at all times, in the Spirit!*

The Word of God instructs us in Jude 1:20, "But ye, beloved, building up yourselves on your most holy faith, praying in the Holy Ghost," praying in tongues overcomes the enemy of your soul.

The Word of God instructs us in 1 Cor. 14:20, "Brethren, be not children in understanding: **howbeit in malice be ye children,** but in understanding, be men", **22** **"Wherefore** tongues are for a sign, **not to them that believe, but to them that believe not".**

THE POWER OF PRAYER IN TONGUES

It is the Holy Ghost who prays God's perfect will for our lives.

Rom 8:26-27

26 Likewise the Spirit also helpeth our infirmities: (inability) for we know not what we should pray for as we ought: **but the Spirit itself maketh** intercession for us **with groanings, which cannot be uttered**

27 And he that searcheth the hearts knoweth what is the mind of the Spirit, because he maketh intercession for the saints **according to the will of God**. (The Holy Ghost searches our hearts.)

How would you like to have a direct line to God, a private line, a secret line that the enemy of our soul doesn't understand?

If we lived in Germany, we would have to learn to speak in a foreign tongue, or if we lived in France, we would have to learn to speak in a foreign tongue, isn't this true? Otherwise we could not communicate.

My dear people, *we are seated with Christ in heavenly places*! We ascended with Jesus and are seated with Him!

Eph. 2:6
And hath raised us up together, and made us sit together in heavenly places in Christ Jesus.
Our Father, who loves us so very much, has given us a heavenly language that the enemy does not understand!
Why? Because we don't know what we should pray for.

The Holy Ghost knows everything about us. The Holy Ghost knows God's will for not only our own lives, but the mind of the Spirit! How?
Because He is supernatural!!
You may be saying to yourself at this very moment, *I don't understand.*
Your mind is not supposed to understand! Why? Because tongues are Supernatural!

1 Cor. 14:14
For if I pray in an unknown tongue, my spirit prayeth, but my understanding is unfruitful.
Why is our understanding unfruitful? Because our spirit is praying!
Our spirit is praying divine mysteries to God Almighty!

1 Cor. 14:2
For he that speaketh in an unknown tongue speaketh not unto men, but unto God: for no man understandeth him; howbeit in the spirit he speaketh mysteries."
God understands every Holy Ghost word spoken in tongues prayed to Him in our heavenly language.
A heavenly language! A gift from our heavenly Father.
Don't forget that God is a Spirit, and is supernatural.

1 Cor. 14:15
What is it then? I will pray with the spirit, and I will pray with the understanding also: I will sing with the spirit, and I will sing with the understanding also.
You see, our mind is our "understander".
You will notice in this verse that Paul the Apostle is showing us that there is a difference between the spirit and the understanding. Or, in other words, the spirit and our mind!
The Apostle is saying I will pray in tongues, and I will pray in the understanding.
What the mind understands is natural language, as tongues are supernatural!
As we pray in the Spirit, by an act of our will, we begin to release our spirit to pray directly to God our Father, through the Holy Ghost within us.
We are then praying mysteries, (divine secrets) to our Father, that are in accordance with God's perfect will!
Now to remove any confusion that you might have in regards to prophesy in the church, there are TWO operations of tongues, notice these verses:

1 Cor. 14:2-3

2   **For he that speaketh in an unknown tongue speaketh not unto men, but unto God**: for no man understandeth him; howbeit in the spirit he speaketh mysteries

3   **But he that prophesieth speaketh unto men** to edification, and exhortation, and comfort.

Verse 2: In our prayer language, we are speaking in an unknown tongue to God, not men!

Verse 3: The gift of prophecy speaks unto men only! (The church)

Cor. 14:4
He that speaketh in an unknown tongue edifieth himself; **but he that prophesieth edifieth the church.**
Again we see two different operations of tongues. As the Word of God instructs us to edify, or build ourselves up, by praying in the Holy Ghost.

Jude 1:20
But ye, beloved, building up yourselves on your most holy faith, praying in the Holy Ghost.
We must have a revelation that we have an enemy that will do anything possible to get us not to pray in our heavenly language.
As we pray in the spirit, the fruits of the old man begin to fall away, replaced by the fruits of the spirit.
The fruits of the old man that don't fall away, are strongholds.
Praying in the spirit is the open channel to receiving what God has for us.
We all have a past that we can't change.
We do have a future that we can change through the power of the Holy Ghost.
The enemy wants to confine our life to the soulish realm to quench our spirit.
We must keep our spirit sweet and soft, we do this by praying in the spirit.
The devil is afraid of the Holy Ghost and tongues of fire. **Tongues consume his evil work by removing hindrances and obstacles in our lives.**
We must remember that Satan is the father of all lies, he is a deceiver, **and hates the church of Jesus Christ!**
Paul the Apostle tells us that he thanked God he spoke in tongues *more than all of us.* The Apostle also had a lot of revelation from the Holy Spirit!

1 Cor. 14:18
I thank my God, I speak with tongues more than ye all.
Then the Apostle tells us in verse 19, "Yet in the church I had rather speak five words with my understanding, that by my voice I might teach others also, than ten thousand words in an unknown tongue".
Why does the Apostle tell us he had rather speak five words with understanding in the church?
Because our mind is our "understander", we couldn't understand him if he spoke in a heavenly language…it's that simple!
Don't let the devil disarm you, he is a deceiver, the father of all lies!

1 Cor. 14:22
Wherefore tongues are for a sign, **not to them that believe, but to them that believe not.**

1 Cor. 14:33

For God is not the author of confusion, but of peace.
Paul knew that the devil would try to confuse us in regards to the doctrine of tongues.

1 Cor. 14:37-39

37 If any man think himself to be a prophet, or spiritual let him acknowledge that the things that I write unto you are the commandments of the Lord but if any man be ignorant, let him be ignorant.
38 Wherefore, brethren, covet to prophesy,
39   and forbid not to speak with tongues.

"Forbid not to speak with tongues."

Satan wants to disarm you, he wants to strip you of your power and authority of the Holy Ghost.

Satan wants to ascend over you and use his deception over you. He is a deceiver!

Luke 11:21-22

21   When a strong man armed keepeth his palace, his goods are in peace
22   But when a stronger than he shall come upon him, and overcome him, he taketh from him all his armor wherein he trusted, and divideth his spoils.

2 Pet. 2:19

For of whom a man is overcome, of the same is he brought in bondage.

2 Tim 3:1

This know also, that in the last days perilous times shall come.

2 Tim 3:5

Having a form of godliness, but denying the power thereof: from such turn away.

The Holy Ghost is the power in the church.
We are to be aggressive towards the enemy.

The Holy Ghost is the supernatural power, the supernatural authority, the supernatural ability, the supernatural anointing, and a supernatural gift from God.

The Holy Ghost is our Comforter, Teacher, Reminder, Counselor, Helper, Intercessor, Advocate, Strengthener, Standby, Revealer of Truth, Guide, and Discernment.

The Holy Ghost gives us the anointing, and does signs and wonders, and defeats the enemy in any test, temptation, or attack from the enemy's camp. Glory to God!

The Holy Ghost can, and does, many things in our lives *for us and through us,* if we allow Him to!

Reread and meditate on this document until you fully understand the content before moving on to document #3.

If you are having a problem understanding the content, pray and ask the Holy Spirit to enlighten the eyes of your understanding.

WATCHMAN RON

Now let us take a look at how the anointing of the Holy Ghost was manifest in Our Lord and Savior Jesus Christ.

Luke 3:22
And the Holy Ghost descended in a bodily shape like a dove upon him, **and a voice came from heaven, which said, Thou art my beloved Son; in thee I am well pleased.**
Here we read in the Word of God how Our Lord Jesus Christ was filled with the Holy Ghost.
Jesus was filled with the Holy Ghost when He was led into the wilderness to be tempted of the devil.

Luke 4:1-3
1   **And Jesus being full of the Holy Ghost** returned from Jordan, and was led by the Spirit into the wilderness
2   Being forty days tempted of the devil. And in those days he did eat nothing: and when they were ended, he afterward hungered
3   **And the devil said unto him,** "If thou be the Son of God, command this stone that it be made bread."

First of all, notice that Jesus is full of the Holy Ghost and power.
He was anointed at the river Jordan.
He was praying and fasting those forty days, the devil said unto Him, (in other words, the devil spoke to Him).
The devil spoke to Jesus the same way the devil speaks to us. How?
Thoughts...fiery darts...thoughts...temptations...thoughts...fiery darts!
Do you get the revelation yet? Jesus and the devil were not flying around the wilderness like Casper the ghost!
The devil attacked the mind of Jesus the same way he attacks our mind, our will, and our emotions.
Jesus was in the wilderness as a man, anointed by the Holy Ghost! He acted by His free will to resist and overcome the enemy of His soul.

Phil. 2:7-8
7   But made himself of no reputation, and took upon him the form of a servant, and was made in the likeness of men:
8   And being found in fashion as a man, **he humbled himself, and became obedient unto death, even the death of the cross. (He was obedient to God by acting upon His will to resist the strategies of the enemy.)**

So what was the temptation?

Luke 4:3

And the devil said unto him, **If thou be the Son of God,** command this stone that it be made bread.

The devil was tempting Jesus to use His *Deity as the Son of God,* instead of a man filled with the Holy Ghost!

What was the answer of Jesus?

Luke 4:4

And Jesus answered him, saying, *It is written* **that man** shall not live by bread alone, but by every word of God.

(Speak the word of God, *an act of our will…*)

Lets go on…are you getting the revelation yet? Glory to God!

Luke 4:5

And the devil, taking him up into an high mountain, shewed unto him all the kingdoms of the world in a moment of time.

Can you imagine in your mind places you have been or would like to go in a moment of time?

My dear people, if our imaginations are a temptation from the devil, don't we sometimes know it?

The word of God tells us to cast down vain imaginations and take them captive!

2 Cor. 10:5

Casting down imaginations, and every high thing that exalteth itself against the knowledge of God, **and bringing into captivity every thought** to the obedience of Christ;

It is the devil who tries to exalt himself against the knowledge (The Word) of God.

Luke 4:6-7

6   **And the devil said unto him,** All this power will I give thee, and the glory of   them: for that is delivered unto me; and to whomsoever I will I give it
7   If thou therefore wilt worship me, all shall be thine.

Again the devil tempts the Son of Man, tempting Him with the kingdoms of this world, if the Son of Man will worship him.
It's no different today, the temptations are the same. Notice that the devil spoke to Him! How?
Thoughts…fiery darts…thoughts…temptations…thoughts…fiery darts!

Luke 4:8
And Jesus answered and said unto him, Get thee behind me, Satan: for it is written, Thou shalt worship the Lord thy God, and him only shalt thou serve (Speak the word of God, an act of our will.)

Luke 4:9-12
9 And he brought him to Jerusalem, and set him on a pinnacle of the temple, and said unto him, **If thou be the Son of God,** cast thyself down from hence:
10 For it is written, He shall give his angels charge over thee, to keep thee:
11 And in their hands they shall bear thee up, lest at any time thou dash thy foot against a stone.
12 And Jesus answering said unto him, It is said, Thou shalt not tempt the Lord thy God.

Luke 4:13

And when the devil had ended all the temptation, he departed from him **for a season.**

please understand that as long as we live on this earth as a man, in this flesh of ours, we are going to have temptations and trials.

We overcome these temptations and trials from the devil the same way Jesus overcame him. **By taking the thought captive, and speaking the Word of God!**

We must disregard feelings of the flesh to be truly victorious in the spiritual realm.

The anointing of the Holy Ghost defeats the enemy in any test, temptation, or attack from the enemy's camp.

Whether it be in our mind, our will, or our emotions!

The enemy works on the mind, will, and emotions.

Our Lord Jesus Christ humbled Himself as a man to show us the way.

Jesus fought the enemy with the Word of God and the Power of the Holy Ghost!

Believers make the mistake of being passive, they are waiting on God to work a miracle in their lives, and God is a miracle working God!

The miracle is the cross, the fact that Jesus rose from the dead, ascended to Heaven, and is seated at the right hand of our Father in heavenly places, where we are seated with Him!

Jesus paid the price for us and said, "it is finished", and gave the authority to us!

Wake up church!
Pick up the sword of the spirit and get the devil off your back! **God has given us the power of the Holy Ghost to defeat the enemy of our soul! Glory to His name! When under attack from the enemy, you will regain your freedom after having resisted his attacks.**
Like Jesus, we are to be aggressive towards the enemy of our soul.
Freedom of spirit is our God-given right, however, we still must use our free will to overcome.
This warfare requires death to self.
If you have given ground to the enemy you must discern the reason why and deal with it.
Normally, it is the old man rising up. After the old man is dealt with, you will be restored to freedom.

Heb. 5:12-14
12   **when for the time ye ought to be teachers, ye have need that one teach you again** which be the first principles of the oracles of God; and are become such as have need of milk, and not of strong meat,
13   For every one that useth milk is unskillful in the word of righteousness: for he is a babe.
14   **But strong meat belongeth to them that are of full age**, even those who by reason of use have their senses exercised to discern both good and evil.

Heb. 6:1-2

1   Therefore leaving the principles of the doctrine of Christ, let us go on unto perfection; not laying again the foundation of repentance from dead works, and of faith toward God,
2   Of the doctrine of baptisms, and of laying on of hands, and of resurrection of the dead, and of eternal judgment

It is time to move into what we are called to do, and operate in the anointing of the Holy Ghost!

Operate in the power of the Holy Ghost!

Operate in the supernatural power of the Holy Ghost!

What do you think His ministry is?
The ministry of the Holy Ghost is the same as it has always been, to operate in supernatural power to defeat the enemy!!
We are the body of Jesus on the earth.
God wants to use us and the Church in power, to defeat the enemy of our soul.

HOWEVER, IT IS AN ACT OF OUR OWN FREE WILL!
We read in Luke 4:14, "And Jesus returned in the power of the Spirit into Galilee: and there went out a fame of him through all the region round about."
If you are abiding in the Holy Ghost, you will move in the power of the Holy Ghost, Jesus practiced abiding in the Holy Ghost. (An act of His will.)

Phil. 2:8
And being found in fashion as a man, **he humbled himself,** and became obedient **unto death, even the death of the cross.**
Jesus was, and is, our example in all things. He walked in the power of the Holy Ghost!

1 Pet. 1:13-14
13 **Wherefore gird up the loins of your mind**, be sober, and hope to the end for the grace that is to be brought unto you at the revelation of Jesus Christ;
14 As obedient children, not fashioning yourselves according to the former lusts in your ignorance…
God has already sent His word to bring us salvation, to heal us, and to overturn situations in our lives.

All of these wonderful blessings come through the power of the BLOOD.

It's time to allow the Holy Ghost to have His way in our lives by maintaining the anointing of the Holy Ghost.

Our Lord Jesus was constantly abiding in prayer to our Father, abiding in His presence in order to maintain the anointing of the Holy Ghost.

THE POWER OF PRAYER

Matt. 14:23
And when he had sent the multitudes away, he went up into a mountain apart to PRAY: **and when the evening was come, he was there alone.**

Matt. 26:36

Then cometh Jesus with them unto a place called Gethsemane, and saith unto the disciples, Sit ye here, while I go and pray yonder.

Luke 6:12
And it came to pass in those days, that he went out into a mountain to pray, and continued all night in prayer to God.
Jesus was maintaining the anointing, **the supernatural anointing, of the Holy Ghost by building Himself up. Praying in the Holy Ghost!!**

Jude 1:20
But ye, beloved, building up yourselves on your most holy faith, praying   in   the Holy Ghost...
We know that Jesus was praying in the Holy Ghost because Jesus was always obedient to the Word of God, **"even unto death". Also, that when we pray in our natural language, our mind (understander) is praying.**
In tongues, our spirit is praying God's perfect will. (Rom. 8:27)
Nor did Jesus want the enemy to understand His private prayer to the Father!

Acts 2:1-4
1   And when the day of Pentecost was fully come, they were all with one accord in one place
2   And suddenly there came a sound from heaven as of a rushing mighty wind, and it filled all the house where they were sitting
3   And there appeared unto them cloven tongues like as of fire, and it sat upon each of them,
4   And they were all filled with the Holy Ghost, and began to speak with other tongues, as the Spirit gave them utterance.
5   With the anointing of the Holy Ghost and tongues of fire, all the children of God in the upper room were filled with the power, ability, and authority of the Holy Ghost. Glory to God!

How do we maintain the anointing, the power, the ability, and authority of the Holy Ghost?

The disciples gave themselves continually to prayer and the study of the word of God!

Acts 6:2-4
2   Then the twelve called the multitude of the disciples unto them, and said, It is not reason that we should leave the word of God, and serve tables
3   Wherefore, brethren, look ye out among you seven men of honest report, **full of the Holy Ghost and wisdom,** whom we may appoint over this business
4   But we will give ourselves continually to prayer, and to the ministry of the word...

The disciple's prayer life, and the prayer life of Jesus, is a MAJOR KEY to maintaining the anointing! (KEYS UNLOCK DOORS!)

Acts 6:4
But we will give ourselves continually to prayer, **and to the ministry of the word.**
This is where most people miss it! Because of Peter's prayer life and dedication to the word, God moved! Remember, it was mostly prayer time and going about doing good, as there were neither Bibles, nor a printing press, to print them on.

The New Testament was being hand written by the Apostles in the form of the gospel and epistles (letters to the churches).

The disciples were built up with the power of the Holy Ghost, from praying in Holy Ghost tongues. Glory!

Jude 1:20

But ye, beloved, building up yourselves on your most holy faith, praying in the Holy Ghost...

Build up your spiritman to become strong in the Spirit, (strong in the anointing of the Holy Ghost), by praying in your heavenly language (in tongues).

The enemy wants to stop you, he wants to disarm you and he doesn't want you strong in the Spirit. You are a threat to him when you have revelation about the power of the Holy Ghost.

The Holy Ghost is a major key to being the overcomer that God has called us to be...to overcome the enemy of our soul!

The disciples had learned a valuable lesson that Jesus had taught them. The anointing and power of the Holy Ghost had to be maintained by close fellowship and communion in prayer by the Holy Ghost. Aren't we called to duplicate Jesus on this earth?

Let's look at some of the deacons that were with the disciples, whom the disciples were teaching, or duplicating, themselves.

Acts 6:5

And the saying pleased the whole multitude: and they chose Stephen, a man full of faith and of the Holy Ghost, and Philip, **and Prochorus, and Nicanor, and Timon, and Parmenas, and Nicolas a proselyte of Antioch:**

Acts 6:8

And Stephen, full of faith and power, did great wonders and miracles among the people.

Acts 6:10

And they were not able to resist the wisdom and the spirit by which he spake...

The Holy Ghost does signs and wonders, and gives us revelation knowledge, when we give Him our will in prayer, (in the spirit), and are obedient to God's will for our lives. (An act of our will.)

Stephen, a man full of faith and of the Holy Ghost, was duplicating the Apostles, who were duplicating Our Lord Jesus Christ!

He is the vine, we are the branches. Praise Him!

Acts 8:5-7

5   Then Philip went down to the city of Samaria, and preached Christ unto them

6   And the people with one accord gave heed unto those things which Philip spake, hearing and seeing the miracles which he did

7   For unclean spirits, crying with loud voice, came out of many that were possessed with them: and many taken with palsies, and that were lame, were healed.

Stephen and Phillip were Deacons in the church.

They had learned how to maintain the anointing of the Holy Ghost from the Apostles, (who learned from Jesus). How to maintain the anointing, just like you are learning right now!

Acts 9:36-41

36 Now there was at Joppa a certain disciple named Tabitha, which by interpretation is called Dorcas: this woman was full of good works and alms, deeds which she did
37 **And it came to pass in those days, that she was sick, and died:** whom when they had washed, they laid her in an upper chamber
38 And forasmuch as Lydda was nigh to Joppa, and the disciples had heard that Peter was there, they sent unto him two men, desiring him that he would not delay to come to them
39 Then Peter arose and went with them When he was come, they brought him into the upper chamber: and all the widows stood by him weeping, and shewing the coats and garments which Dorcas made, while she was with them
40 **But Peter put them all forth, and kneeled down, and prayed;** and turning him to the body said, Tabitha, arise **And she opened her eyes:** and when she saw Peter, she sat up
41 **And he gave her his hand, and lifted her up,** and when he had called the saints and widows, presented her alive.

Peter raised Tabitha from the dead when he spoke in authority with the anointing of the Holy Ghost. The Holy Ghost is our ability, authority, and our anointing.

Mark 16:17-20

17 And these signs shall follow them that believe; In my name shall they cast out devils; they shall speak with new tongues;
18 They shall take up serpents; and if they drink any deadly thing, it shall not hurt them; they shall lay hands on the sick, and they shall recover
19 So then after the Lord had spoken unto them, he was received up into heaven, and sat on the right hand of God
20 And they went forth, and preached every where, the Lord working with them, and confirming the word with signs following. Amen

This is one of the very last things spoken to the church at the ascension of Jesus. Don't you think it is important, as it was the last thing Our Lord told us? It is very important to Jesus, as we are His body, His hands, His feet, His mouth, His voice…in the earth.
Most Christians that are filled with the power and anointing of the Holy Ghost are not aware of the authority that we possess. Nor do they know how to maintain the authority and anointing of the Holy Ghost! The believer today is trying to "believe" for what already belongs to them.
All we need to do is to maintain the "fire" of the Holy Ghost. It is the anointing of the Holy Ghost that destroys the yoke of bondage.

Isa. 10:27

And the yoke shall be destroyed because of the anointing. (of the Holy Ghost)

Isa. 28:9

Whom shall he teach knowledge? And whom shall he make to understand doctrine?
Them that are weaned from the milk, **and drawn from the breasts.**

"It is time to get off of the milk!" (An act of our will.)

Jer. 23:29

Is not my word like as a fire? saith the LORD; **and like a hammer that breaketh the rock in pieces?**
A fire consumes anything in its path, a hammer breaks up rocks (resistance.) Maintaining the anointing of the Holy Ghost is like keeping a fire going strong. A fire can die down to an ember if it's not maintained, a fire can get so low you can't feel any warmth anymore. The fire of the Holy Ghost has to be maintained! Begin to build up the fire of the Holy Ghost, begin to maintain that Holy Ghost fire that's in you!

Jude 1:20
But ye, beloved, building up yourselves on your most holy faith, praying   in   the Holy Ghost...
With the Holy Ghost and fire, Jesus becomes alive, Jesus becomes real, Jesus fills your heart, Jesus fills your life.
With the Holy Ghost and fire, heaven opens the gates wide, the anointing flows, everything the Holy Ghost touches lives, the Glory of God will penetrate your spirit.
It is time to get off of the milk. **It is time to stop being passive. It is time we go on to perfection. It is time to pick up the sword of the Spirit and get the devil off of your back!**

Heb 6:1-2

1   Therefore leaving the principles of the doctrine of Christ, **let us go on unto perfection**; not laying again the foundation of repentance from dead works, and of faith toward God,

2   2   of the doctrine of baptisms, and of laying on of hands, and of resurrection of the dead, and of eternal judgment.

Rom. 12:1-2

1   I beseech you therefore, brethren, by the mercies of God, that ye present your bodies a living sacrifice, holy, acceptable unto God, which is your reasonable service. (An act of our will.)

2   **And be not conformed to this world: but be ye transformed by the renewing of your mind**, (An act of our will) that ye may prove what is that   good, and acceptable, and perfect, will of God.

We need a greater power than that of the "evil one", who can tempt and influence our flesh to be able to live a sanctified life, holy and acceptable unto God.

God knew that the enemy of our soul would be out in the open in these last days.

Believers need God's power to enable them to stand against the power of evil in these last days.

When we give God not only our heart (spirit man), through salvation of the cross, but also our flesh (mind, will, emotions), the Holy Ghost can and does move through us to do the sanctifying work needed in our lives, by removing hindrances in our lives.

This is done when we begin to give the Holy Ghost place in our lives (**an act of our will**).

The Holy Ghost brings us into perfection and maturity by overcoming hindrances that so easily beset us.

Heb. 12:1

Wherefore seeing we also are compassed about with so great a cloud of witnesses, **let us lay aside every weight, and the sin which doth so easily beset us,** and let us run with patience the race that is set before us. (**An act of our will.**)

The Holy Ghost is the one who brings the Word of God into manifestation in our lives, so that we can become the overcomer that the Bible talks about.

To be an overcomer is also an act of our will, not just faith, all by itself!

Heb. 11:7

By faith Noah, being warned of God of things not seen as yet, moved with fear, **prepared an ark to the saving of his house**; by which he condemned the world, and became heir of the righteousness which is by faith. (**An act of Noah's will.**)

Heb. 11:8

By faith Abraham, when he was called to go out into a place which he should after receive for an inheritance, **obeyed;** and he went out, not knowing whither he went. (**An act of Abraham's will.**)

Heb. 11:11

Through faith also Sara herself received strength to conceive seed, and was delivered of a child when she was past age, because she judged him faithful who had promised. (**An act of Sara's will, as Isaac was not incarnate!**)

Phil. 2:5

Let this mind be in you, which was also in Christ Jesus:

Phil. 2:8

And being found in fashion as a man, he humbled himself, and became obedient unto death, even the death of the cross." (**An act of His will.**)

All three of these faithful people of God, plus our beloved Lord Jesus Christ, believed God's promise for their lives.

They, by an act of their own free will, were used by God to fulfill these promises that changed history!

We also have a promise from God Almighty, through the lips of our Lord and Savior, Jesus Christ, who spoke only the words of Almighty God!

Luke 24:49

And, behold, **I send the promise of my Father upon you:** but tarry ye in the city of Jerusalem, until ye be endued with power from on high.

We have a promise from our heavenly Father that He will endue us with power from on high!

If we were not involved in a battle of supernatural proportions, *why would we need to be endued with power?*

Our Lord and Savior came to this earth by crossing over from the supernatural (Spirit realm), to the natural realm (where we are), to tell us the truth, and how it really is, so we would be able to cope in this life, and be an overcomer, as He overcame. (An act of His will.)

John 8:32

And ye shall know the truth, and the truth shall make you free.

Jesus tells us in John 10:10, "The thief cometh not, but for to steal, and to kill, and to destroy: I am come that they might have life, and that they might have it more abundantly".

If you are not having life, and having it more abundantly, then the thief   (Satan and his hosts) have come to steal, and to kill, and to destroy!

Priests… you have the authority to go after the thief.

The devil and his army steal, kill, and destroy, through deception!

Satan is a deceiver, he is the father of all lies. Don't ever forget who your enemy is, and that we are in a spiritual battle!

Satan and his army try and deceive us through existing strongholds, getting us to dwell upon a thought or a temptation that he has implanted in our minds.

His goal is to get us to act upon the temptation, and fall through sin, or to dwell upon the thought, so he can build stronger strongholds in our lives that will become hindrances to the Holy Ghost.

When these hindrances are in place, the Holy Ghost cannot move through us, as we have surrendered our ground to the enemy, by an act of our own free will.

If, however, you have given ground to the enemy, you must recognize the reason why and deal with the situation.

Normally, it is the old man rising up. After you deal with the situation, according to God's instructions, you will be restored to freedom.

Remember God has given us a free will to choose whom we will serve.

The enemy wants to confine you to the soulish realm to quench your spirit.

We must mobilize Holy Ghost spiritual power to remove the enemy.

Satan and his army of fallen angels are trying to resurrect the old man that died on the cross with Jesus!

The enemy is using the vehicle of old strongholds to tempt your flesh, to resurrect the old rubbish of your past that you left at the cross of Jesus Christ.

Strongholds of: Sexual Addiction, Pornography, Lust, Anger, Anxiety, Bitterness, Condemnation, Confusion, Covetousness, Criticism, Depression, Discouragement, Disease, Disobedience, Distress, Doubt, Fear, Greed, Guilt, Heartache, Impatience,

Inferiority, Insecurity, Judgment, Lying, Low Self-Esteem, Materialism, Mistrust, Negativism, Obesity, Oppression, Past Hurts, Poverty, Pride, Problems, Rebellion, Rejection, Religion, Revenge, Selfishness, Self-Pity, Shame, Sickness, Sorrow, Stress, Spirit of Heaviness, Strife, Temptation, Thievery, Timidity, Unbelief, Unrighteousness, Violence, Witchcraft, Worry…

Father: I declare, by an act of my free will, to know truth and to obey truth, which is the word of God.

I declare to obey God's will.

I declare to resist Satan's will.

I declare to exercise my own will.

I choose freedom.

I want liberty.

I refuse to be passive.

I will sever every relationship with darkness. I will have freedom.
For it is written:

Rev. 12:11
And they overcame him by the blood of the Lamb, and by the word of their testimony; and they loved not their   lives unto the death.

Reread and meditate on this document until you fully understand the entire content before moving on to document #4.

If you are having a problem understanding the content, pray and ask the Holy Spirit to enlighten the eyes of your understanding.

THE POWER OF THE RESURRECTION

Rom. 6:6
Knowing this, that our old man is crucified with him, **that the body of sin might be destroyed, that henceforth** we should not serve sin.
(An act of our will.)

Rom. 6:11
Likewise, reckon ye also yourselves to be dead indeed unto sin, but alive unto God through Jesus Christ our Lord. (An act of our will)

2 Cor. 5:17
Therefore if any man be in Christ, he is a new creature: old things are passed away; behold all things are become new. We are a new creature in Christ Jesus, the old man is passed away, all things are new! The old man is dead! The old man is dead! The old man is dead! The old man is dead!
Satan tries to resurrect the old man, using the vehicle of strongholds and thoughts of past sin and past pleasures of the flesh, addictions of the flesh, past habits, lust of the flesh, lust of the eyes, bondage of all sorts, and the carnal mind.

Gal. 5:16-21
16 This I say then, walk in the Spirit, and ye shall not fulfil the lust of the flesh,
17 **for the flesh lusteth against the Spirit, and the Spirit against the flesh:** and these are contrary the one to the other: so that ye cannot do the things that ye would.
18 **But, if ye be led of the Spirit, ye are not under the law.**
19 Now, the works of the flesh are manifest, which are these; adultery, fornication, uncleanness, **lasciviousness, (tending to excite lustful desires)**
20 Idolatry, witchcraft, hatred, variance, emulations, wrath, strife, seditions, heresies,
21 Envyings, murders, drunkenness, revellings, and such like of which I tell you before, as I have also told you in time past, that they, which do such things, shall not inherit the kingdom of God.

Paul the Apostle speaks of the works of the flesh, saying they are the product of a corrupt nature.
Some are sin against the seventh commandment, (such as adultery, fornication, uncleanness, lustful desires), by which are meant not only the gross acts of these sins, but also such thoughts, words, and actions, as have a tendency towards sin.
Some are sin against the first and second commandments, such as idolatry and witchcraft.
Others are sin against our neighbor, and contrary to the law of brotherly love, (such as hatred, anger, wrath, strife), which too often bring about rebellion, or opinions opposed to doctrines of the church, (envy), and sometimes break out into murder.
Others are sins against our self, such as drunkenness.
There is a struggle between the old nature and the new nature, the old man and the new man, the remainders of sin and the beginnings of grace; and this, Christians must expect, will be our exercise as long as we live in this world. Those who are in the flesh cannot please God, which seals the fate of the fleshy.

Rom. 8:8

So then, they that are in the flesh cannot please God.

So closely is flesh linked with lust that the word of God often refers to lusts of the flesh.

Gal. 5:16

This I say then, Walk in the Spirit, and ye shall not fulfill the lust of the flesh.

The flesh in a born again Christian is the same as the sinner. For, in the new birth, the flesh is not transformed. The new birth does not influence the flesh. The flesh remains *as is*.

We ourselves, through the power of the Holy Spirit and following the guidelines God has given us, must overcome the flesh. The flesh demands full control... so does the Spirit.

The flesh desires to have man attached to it, while the Holy Spirit wants us to be subject to the things of God.

The nature of the flesh is from the first Adam. The nature of the second Adam is from Jesus. The first is earthly, the second heavenly.

1 Cor. 15:45

And so it is written, the first man Adam was made a living soul; the last Adam was made a quickening spirit.

Flesh focuses all things upon self.

The Holy Spirit focuses upon Jesus.

The flesh wants us to sin when we are tempted by evil.

The Holy Spirit leads us to righteousness

When the flesh begins to wrestle with our spirit, we will begin to discern that housed within us are two directions that we can yield to.

It is as though there are two different persons fighting for control of our soul. This is an incredible experience.

When we are born again, we must have the revelation that we have been crucified with Christ.

Rom. 6:6-8

6 **Knowing this, that our old man is crucified with him,** that the body of sin might be destroyed, that henceforth, we should not serve sin.

7 For he that is dead is free from sin.

8 Now, if we be dead with Christ, we believe that we shall also live with him.

THE OLD MAN IS DEAD, THE OLD MAN IS DEAD. THE OLD MAN IS DEAD, THE OLD MAN IS DEAD!

If many worldly habits cling to your life, then you are still of the flesh.

When sin is in control, the flesh exhibits its strength in self-defense.

It opposes anything that may interfere with its comfort and pleasure.

Most sin springs from self-interest, self-existence, self-glory, self-opinion, and selfish motives.

It is abnormal for a born again Christian to remain for a long period in the flesh, fail to subdue sin, and live a double minded life.

James 1:8

A double-minded man is unstable in all his ways.

Works of the flesh may be divided into five groups

1. Sin that defiles the body.
Immorality

Impurity

Morally unrestrained, especially in sexual activity.
These particular sins actually vex our soul, which causes us to be tormented by evil
spirits. If you have not experienced this manifestation, you have not overcome the
flesh.
This manifestation can occur in seeing or hearing immoral activity.
If we look at Lot in the city of Sodom and Gomorrah:

2 Pet 2:7-8
7   And delivered just Lot, vexed with the filthy conversation of the wicked:
8   (For that righteous man dwelling among them, in seeing and hearing, vexed his
     righteous soul from day to day with their unlawful deeds;)

   2. Sinful communications with satanic forces, such as idolatry or
      sorcery.

   3. Sinful temper such as anger, strife, jealousy, bitterness, hatred,
      hostility.

   4. Religious cults, selfishness, envy.

   5. Tending to excite lustful desires, also drunkenness and
      carousing.

Those who do these are of the flesh. **A Born Again Christian** should be able to
recognize his own weakness of the flesh. **Only by overcoming our flesh may we truly**
be free in the Spirit.

The fact that we have been crucified with Christ on the cross means that we are not
crucified again. We must overcome the flesh as the enemy tries to resurrect it.

If we, therefore, desire to be led by the Holy Spirit, and to be freed from the oppression
of the flesh, we must put to death the wicked deeds of the flesh and walk according to the
Holy Spirit. We have the possibility of sinning, **but we must not sin.**

The Lord Jesus died for us and crucified our flesh with himself on the cross. The
Holy Spirit dwells in us to give us the revelation of what the Lord Jesus truly
accomplished. **The presence of the flesh is our invitation to overcome.** If we persist
in living by the flesh when we know truth, it is because we want to be fleshy.

Always remember that the flesh makes SELF the center and elevates self-will above
God's will. It may even serve God, but always according to its own ideals, not God's.
Self is the principle behind every action!

Self-confidence and self-reliance are the traits of the good works of the flesh.

Pride is self-importance. It is impossible for the flesh to lean upon God.

The flesh is too impatient to tolerate any delay. As long as the flesh thinks it is strong, it will never depend upon God. The flesh will always look for a way out. Whenever a heart of utter trust is lacking, there is the labor of flesh.

The old man is willing to do anything, even submit to God, if it is permitted to live and be active. The flesh remains unshaken in its ability.

Gal 3:3

Are ye so foolish? Having begun in the Spirit, are ye now made perfect by the flesh?

Rom 8:5-6

6   For they that are after the flesh do mind the things of the flesh; but they that are after the Spirit the things of the Spirit. (An act of our will.)

7   For to be carnally minded is death; but to be spiritually minded is life and peace. (An act of our will)

2 Cor. 10:3-5
3   **For though we walk in the flesh, we do not war after the flesh:**
4   For the weapons of our warfare are not carnal, but mighty through God to the pulling down of strong holds;
5   Casting down imaginations, (An act of our will) and every high thing that exalteth itself against the knowledge (word) of God, and bringing into captivity every thought (an act of our will) to the obedience of Christ; (the Word).

The mind can be addicted to thoughts that are pleasing to the flesh, (such as past sexual sin), or desires, (such as drugs, alcohol, or pornography). According to the Word of God, the mind is the battlefield where Satan and his evil spirits come with lies to deceive us to stop the truth of God's Word.

The enemy wants to keep us in bondage to the past by deceiving us and keeping our minds captured. Satan will use oppression or depression to captivate and disable us so we are not able to function mentally. Oppression or depression creates a feeling of heaviness. We must be able to recognize this heaviness and realize it is from the enemy. We must come against this heaviness from the enemy using the instructions God has given to us through His word.

Other times Satan may use confusion to try to hinder you. If our mind is in captivity, so is our will. And although we are saved by the grace of God, we are still bound.

We should always feel freedom of the spirit within ourselves, which is the opposite of oppression or depression. Our freedom of spirit is a God-given right that Jesus has already shed His blood for.

2 Cor. 10:3-5
3   For though we walk in the flesh, we do not war after the flesh:
4   (For the weapons of our warfare are not carnal, but mighty through God to the pulling down of strong holds ;)
5   Casting down imaginations, and every high thing that exalteth itself against the knowledge of God, and bringing into captivity every thought to the obedience of Christ;

The Word of God likens man's reasoning and arguments to the enemy's stronghold.

The Word of God pictures the mind as being held by the enemy and must be broken into, and taken captive, by waging war. The Word of God plainly shows us that the mind is the scene of a battle where evil spirits clash with God.

2 Cor. 4:4
In whom the god of this world hath blinded the minds of them which believe not, lest the light of the glorious gospel of Christ, who is the image of God, should shine unto them.

Cor. 4:4 declares that Satan holds on to our minds by making it blind.

The eye of our mind has been covered by Satan. The mind becomes hardened and deceived before we are saved. This is the reason we still walk down the same old path after we are born again. These are strongholds. Our mind is still set on things of the flesh.

Please notice the prayer prayed for the church at Ephesus by Paul the Apostle.

Eph. 1:17-18
17 That the God of our Lord Jesus Christ, the Father of glory, may give unto you the spirit of wisdom and revelation in the knowledge of him:
18 **The eyes of your understanding being enlightened**; that ye may know what is the hope of his calling, and what the riches of the glory of his inheritance in the saints…

The eyes of our understanding need to be enlightened, because the eye of our mind has been blinded by Satan. Although we are born again, we still have to overcome the strongholds of the old man through spiritual warfare.

Please note that if you have a loved one that is born again and bound, pray that the eyes of their mind will be enlightened to the truth of God's word in regards to a stronghold in their life that they don't recognize.
Yes, we must overcome, however we must first have the revelation to fight the enemy of our soul and not be passive.

Rom. 8:7
Because the carnal mind is enmity (hostile) against God, for it is not subject to the law of God, neither indeed can be.

When our mind set on the flesh, it is hostile to God. When we compare the mind to an enemy's stronghold, the Word of God implies that Satan and his evil spirits already have established a deep relationship with the minds of men. Satan and his evil spirits are using the mind to imprison their captives. Through our minds, they can influence our thoughts, which in turn influence our will. All reasoning and arguments against the knowledge of God, "the Word of God", are the fortresses of the enemy. Every temptation that Satan entices man with is presented to the mind in the form of thoughts and fiery darts.
In order to use our body, our flesh, the enemy must present the temptation to our mind first. Satan must get our consent first, as we have a free will and have been set free at the cross. Satan and his evil host can only tempt us. Temptations and thoughts cannot be separated.

We must post a Watchman at all times to guard against the powers of darkness...against temptations to sin.

Matt 26:41
Watch and pray that ye enter not into temptation: the spirit indeed is willing, but the flesh is weak.
The mind suffers the onslaught of the powers of darkness.
Attacking the mind is the easiest avenue for them to accomplish their purpose. What is their purpose?

John 10:10
The thief cometh not, but for to steal, to kill, and to destroy: I am come that they might have life, and that they might have it more abundantly.

They come to steal, kill and destroy our free will.
Eve's heart was sinless, and yet she received the evil thoughts of Satan in the Garden of Eden. She fell through deception and reasoning, and fell into the snare of the enemy. It is possible for a child of God to have a new life, and a new heart, and still be born again and bound, resurrected and not yet released, a prisoner
in the Promised Land. This is the reason why we have seen great men of God fall to sexual sin, or some other lust of the flesh. The simple fact is that their hearts were renewed but their minds still had strongholds of the enemy at work.
Continue to pray that our minds will be enlightened, for God to shine His light into our darkness. God has the desire to restore our minds to what He has created us to be. To be able to glorify Him, not only with our heart, but also with our minds.

Rom. 12:2
And be not conformed to this world: but be ye transformed by the renewing of your mind, that ye may prove what is that good, and acceptable, and perfect, will of God.
Who controls your mind? Is it you? Is it God? If it is neither you, nor God, then who is it?
The truth is, because we have been given a free will, God's intention is for us to be in control of ourselves. You will find that after you have truly overcome the enemy, you begin to notice that you will be restored to having clear thoughts.
You will also notice that those frequent thoughts and fiery darts from your past strongholds do not come around anymore.
How sweet it is!

A born again Christian should ask himself:
Are these my thoughts? Is it I who is thinking?
A born again Christian should determine if it is himself who is doing the thinking. We must never lose the element of our God-given free will.
If you have not originated the idea, but, on the contrary, oppose the thought, and yet the thought still abides in your mind, you can assume that the thought has come from the enemy's camp.

John 13:2
And supper being ended, the devil having now put into the heart of Judas Iscariot, Simon's son, to betray him;
The Word of God shows us that the powers of darkness are able to impart thoughts into our minds.

Luke 8:12
Those by the way side are they that hear; then cometh the devil, and taketh away the word out of their hearts, lest they should believe and be saved.
The Word of God shows us that the devil can also remove what we should remember.
Showing us a two-fold operation of evil spirits upon the mind of man.
When we give ground to the enemy of our soul through our mind, the enemy will immediately seize upon our will to bring his will to pass, which is to sin against a Holy God.
The flesh gives ground to the enemy.
If our mind is not renewed to the Word of God, we are open to the wiles (strategies) of the enemy. All sin furnishes territory for the onslaught of evil spirits. If a born again Christian cherishes past sin in his heart, he is loaning his mind to evil spirits for their use, as long as sins of the past linger, are allowed to persist, and are allowed to remain in the heart. That is precisely how long the evil spirits work at capturing your free will to get you to sin against God.
Once you allow a thought to linger and to stay from past sin, you will find the thought more difficult to overcome the next time it raises its ugly head. Remember that the thought is a temptation from the enemy.
The enemy is very persistent, as he wants you to serve him. Satan wants to pull you back into darkness. Satan knows what the weak link is in the chain of your life, after all, he is the one who put it there in the first place.

Matt. 12:25-30
25 And Jesus knew their thoughts, and said unto them, every kingdom divided against itself is brought to desolation; and every city or house divided against itself shall not stand:
26 And if Satan cast out Satan, he is divided against himself; how shall then his kingdom stand?
27 And if I by Beelzebub cast out devils, by whom do your children castthem out? Therefore, they shall be your judges
28 28 But if I cast out devils by the Spirit of God, **then the kingdom of God is come unto you**
29 29 Or else how can one enter into a strong man's house, and spoil his goods, except he first bind the strong man? And then he will spoil   his house
30 He that is not with me is against me; and he that gathereth not with me scattereth abroad.

My dear people, how can unrepented sin cast out sexual addiction? How can self-pity cast out fear? How can guilt cast out oppression? How can anger cast out insecurity? How can torment cast out hate? How can criticism cast out judgmentalism? How can disobedience cast out guilt? How can condemnation cast out sickness and disease? How can prejudice cast out hate? How can negativism cast out doubt and unbelief?

HOW CAN SATAN CAST OUT SATAN?

Matt. 12:26
And if Satan cast out Satan, he is divided against himself; how shall then his kingdom stand?

Matt. 12:30
He that is not with me is against me; and he that gathereth not with me scattereth abroad.

This is how Satan and his hosts disarm you, the church, and me! Now you know why Jesus warned us that a house divided against itself cannot stand! Satan sends thoughts, temptations, and evil spirits to steal, to kill, and destroy our anointing, by using strategies to get us to use our own free will to defeat us.

Rev. 12:10
And I heard a loud voice saying in heaven, Now is come salvation, and strength, and the kingdom of our God, and the power of his Christ: for the accuser of our brethren is cast down, which accused them before our God day and night.
Satan is the accuser of the brethren. The only way that Lucifer (Satan) can accuse us, is when we have given him permission to do so, by an act of our own free will. We do this when we fall to his strategy.
WHEN YOU CHANGE YOUR POSITION, GOD WILL CHANGE YOUR SITUATION!

Eph. 2:4-6
4   But God, who is rich in mercy, for his great love wherewith he loved us,
5   Even when we were dead in sin, hath quickened us together with Christ, (by grace ye are saved;)
6   And hath raised us up together, and made us sit together in heavenly places in Christ Jesus:

How do we maintain our seat in heavenly places?

How do we maintain the anointing of the Holy Ghost?

How do we walk in the power of the Holy Ghost?

How do we overcome the enemy of our soul?

How do we keep the enemy under our feet?

By an act of our own, God-given, free will!

Eph. 6:12-18
12   For we wrestle not against flesh and blood, but against principalities, against powers, against the rulers of the darkness of this world, against spiritual wickedness in high places
13   **Wherefore, take unto you the whole armor of God that** ye may be able to withstand in the evil day, and having done all, to stand
14   Stand therefore, having your loins girt about with truth, and having on the breastplate of righteousness;
15   And your feet shod with the preparation of the gospel of peace;
16   Above all, taking the shield of faith, wherewith ye shall be able to quench all the fiery darts of the wicked...(THOUGHTS, FIERY DARTS)
17   And take the helmet of salvation, **and the sword of the Spirit,** which is the word of God:

18　**Praying always with all prayer and supplication in the Spirit,** and　watching thereunto with all **perseverance** and supplication for all　saints, (pray in the Spirit, always)

The act of perseverance… A continued, patient effort. An act of your free will.

Now let's pick up the sword of the Spirit.　If you will notice, there is no scabbard to put away or to store your sword, **we are to never lay our sword down.　Does the enemy ever put his weapons away?　No, the old devil works twenty-four hours a day if we let him!**

Example: Worry is meditation from the enemy's camp, the Word of God gives us instructions:

Phil. 4:8
Finally, brethren, whatsoever things are true, whatsoever things are honest, whatsoever things are just, whatsoever things are pure, whatsoever things are lovely, whatsoever things are of good report; if there be any virtue, and if there be any praise, think on these things.

AN ACT OF OUR WILL

Prov. 4:20-27
20　My son, attend to my words; incline thine ear unto my sayings
21　Let them not depart from thine eyes; keep them in the midst of thine heart
22　For they are life unto those that find them, and health to all their flesh
23　Keep thy heart with all diligence; for out of it are the issues of life
24　Put away from thee a froward mouth, and perverse lips put far from thee
25　Let thine eyes look right on, and let thine eyelids look straight before thee
26　Ponder the path of thy feet, and let all thy ways be established
27　Turn not to the right hand nor to the left: remove thy foot from evil

WHY IS THE WORD OF GOD SO IMPORTANT?　BECAUSE IT IS SUPERNATURAL!

What weapon did Jesus use in the wilderness against the enemy of His soul?　THE POWER OF THE WORD OF GOD.

Jesus spoke the Word of God when He was confronted by the thoughts and fiery darts of the devil, showing us, by example, how to defeat the enemy when he tries to ascend over us, by trying to invade our mind, will, or emotions.　The Word of God keeps the devil at bay when we speak it from our lips!

Matt. 11:12
And from the days of John the Baptist until now the kingdom of heaven suffereth violence, and the violent take it by force"
[DIVINE POWER, THE WORD OF GOD]

Heb. 11:3
Through faith we understand that the worlds were framed by the word of God, **so that things which are seen were not made of things which do appear.**

Heb. 1:3

Who being the brightness of his glory, and the express image of his person, and upholding all things by the word of his power, **when he had by himself purged our sins, sat down on the right hand of the Majesty on high;**

Heb. 4:12
For the word of God is quick, and powerful, and sharper than any two-edged sword, **piercing even to the dividing asunder of soul and spirit, and of the joints and marrow, and is a discerner of the thoughts and intents of the heart.**

John 6:63
It is the spirit that quickeneth; the flesh profiteth nothing: the words that I speak unto you, they are spirit, and they are life.

Prov. 4:20
My son, attend to my words; incline thine ear unto my sayings.

Prov. 4:22
For they are life unto those that find them, and health to all their flesh.

Jer. 1:12
Then said the LORD unto me, Thou hast well seen: for I will hasten my word to perform it.

Our heavenly Father watches over His Word to perform it when we wield the sword of the Spirit.
The Prophet Jeremiah was set over nations and over kingdoms, to root out, to pull down, to destroy, to throw down the kingdoms of darkness, then God told him to build and to plant the kingdom of light, with God's Word.

Jer. 1:10
See, I have this day set thee over the nations and over the kingdoms, to root out, and to pull down, and to destroy, and to throw down, to build, and to plant.

Jer.1:12
Then said the LORD unto me, Thou hast well seen: for I will hasten my word to perform it.
We are to root out, to pull down, to destroy, and to throw down the kingdoms of darkness that have infiltrated our minds. And then we are to build and to plant the kingdom of light in our minds with the Word of God. (It is written)

Acts 2 17-18 (The Prophet Joel speaking of the last days)
17   And it shall come to pass in the last days, saith God, I will pour out of my Spirit upon all flesh: and your sons and your daughters **shall prophesy,** (shall **declare)** and your young men shall see visions, and your old men shall dream dreams:
18   And on my servants and on my handmaidens I will pour out in those days of my Spirit; and they **shall prophesy: (shall declare)** (It is written)

PROPHECY, PROPHESY, PROPHESYING

Prophecy is not necessarily, nor even primarily, foretelling. It is the declaration of that which cannot be known by natural means. (Matt 26:68)

Prophecy is the forth telling of the will of God, whether with reference to the past, the present, or the future. (See Gen. 20:7)

The Prophet Joel is telling us that in the last days that our sons and daughters shall declare... *and God's servants and handmaidens Shall declare... God's Word*, (past, present, and future), into the situations around us. (It is written.)

When Jesus was in the wilderness, He took every thought captive, every temptation to the Word of God. By an act of His own free will. He declared God's Word, (truth) into the situation, stopping the devil in his tracks.

When Jesus said, "It is written", He was wielding the sword of the Spirit! Jesus was showing us by example how to overcome, using God's Word, under the anointing of the Holy Ghost!

2 Pet. 2:19
for of whom a man is overcome, of the same is he brought in bondage.

Eph. 4:22-27
22 That ye put off concerning the former conversation the old man, which is corrupt according to the deceitful lusts;
23 And be renewed in the spirit of your mind;
24 **And that ye put on the new man,** which after God is created in righteousness and true holiness.
27 Neither give place to the devil.

WINNING THE BATTLE IS NOT THE DIFFICULT PART!

IT IS RECOGNIZING YOUR WEAPONS!

IT IS RECOGNIZING THE BATTLE!

IT IS RECOGNIZING THE ENEMY!

Reread and meditate on this document until you fully understand its entire contents before moving on to document #5.

If you are having a problem understanding the content, pray and ask the Holy Spirit to enlighten the eyes of your understanding.

WATCHMAN RON

Too many Christians want to get involved in the action of overcoming their stronghold without first submitting themselves to the discipline necessary to be equipped for spiritual battle. You must understand how each spiritual key and each spiritual move operate in order to overcome the enemy of your. There is a divine order for these weapons to be used in spiritual battle.

The first spiritual move is to always repent of any sin that is resident in your soul on a daily basis whether in thought, word or deed. Repentance is God's grace and mercy in action removing hindrances that will stop the flow of the spirit.

The second spiritual move is the in filling of the Holy Ghost to receive the power of the Holy Ghost. Without the in filling of the Holy Ghost you have no power to overcome the enemy.

The third spiritual move is praying in the spirit, building ourselves up in the Holy Ghost. The purpose of praying in the spirit is to build ourselves up to get strong in the spirit. We must be strong in the spirit before we enter into battle with the enemy.

The forth spiritual move is maintaining the fire and anointing of the Holy Ghost by praying in the spirit. We must maintain the fire, the anointing, to walk continuously in the power of the Holy Ghost.

The fifth spiritual move is the power of the resurrection. We must have the revelation that our old man is crucified with Jesus and that the old man is dead.

Each spiritual move, each spiritual key, has a purpose and is needed to be able to spiritually overcome strongholds and the wills of the flesh. True freedom is incredible, but it takes a commitment to God, perseverance, and an act of your free will to experience total freedom. Satan has stolen our past – he wants to steal our future.

The book of Revelation is the revealing of our Lord Jesus Christ.

Rev 1:1

The Revelation of Jesus Christ, which God gave unto him, to show unto his servants things which must shortly come to pass; and he sent and signified it by his angel unto his servant John:

If you have a red-letter edition of the Bible, you will notice that the letters to the churches were spoken by Jesus and recorded by John the Apostle.

The Greek word for *overcome* in Chapters Two and Three of the book of Revelation is the word "Nikao", it means *to conquer*.

We are to conquer the strongholds and wills of the flesh in this life to become the overcomer Jesus has called us to be.

The word of God is our agent, or sword, that fights our battle for us. The "enemy" is anything that *keeps us in bondage* to something that Jesus has already set us free from.

The enemy must bow his knee to the Word of God, the Name of Jesus, the Blood of the Lamb, and the Power of the Holy Ghost. Winning the battle is not the difficult part, for he is a defeated foe! The difficult part is *recognizing the battle, the thoughts, the temptations, the fiery darts*, as these thoughts may have become a stronghold in our lives, and we may not recognize them as the enemy. Strongholds can become so engrained in our thought life that we perceive them as normal. Or we may have become passive about them and accept them as normal. In either case they are not normal if they are contrary to the word of God.

How do you recognize them? First of all, you probably already know what they are...if you don't, when you begin to pray in the Holy Ghost for any length of time, they will surface as you are praying! They will try to overcome you through the same thought pattern and temptations that may have held you in bondage to the enemy before you were saved. These are strongholds of the enemy that need to be destroyed! These are the strongholds that must be overcome, to become what Jesus has called us to be in the Book of Revelation.

Rev. 2:7
He that hath an ear, let him hear what the Spirit saith unto the churches; to him that overcometh will I give to eat of the tree of life, which is in the midst of the paradise of God.

Rev. 2:11
He that hath an ear, let him hear what the Spirit saith unto the churches; he that overcometh shall not be hurt of the second death.

Rev. 2:17
He that hath an ear, let him hear what the Spirit saith unto the churches; to him that overcometh will I give to eat of the hidden manna, and will give him a white stone, and in the stone a new name written, which no man knoweth saving he that receiveth   it.

Rev. 2:26
And he that overcometh, and keepeth my works unto the end, to him will I give power over the nations:

Rev. 3:5
He that overcometh, the same shall be clothed in white raiment; and I will not blot out his name out of the book of life, but I will confess his name before my Father, and before his angels.

Rev. 3:12
Him that overcometh will I make a pillar in the temple of my God, and he shall go no more out: and I will write upon him the name of my God, and the name of the city of my God, which is new Jerusalem, which cometh down out of heaven from my God: and I will write upon him my new name.

Rev. 3:21
To him that overcometh will I grant to sit with me in my throne, even as I also overcame, and am set down with my Father in his throne.

Rev. 21:7
He that overcometh shall inherit all things; and I will be his God, and he shall be my son.

What does Jesus *want us to overcome* that Jesus *asks us to "hear* what the Spirit of God says to the church"? What does Jesus *want us to overcome,* that He has told the New Testament church SEVEN times within 2 chapters in the book of Revelation, and also at the end of the book of Revelation? We are to overcome flesh, sin and the devil in this life. Today...now.

Heb. 12:1
Let us lay aside every weight, every hindrance, which doth easily beset us Let us run with patience the race that is set before us.

Let us overcome flesh, sin, and the devil. It is the Holy Ghost, and God's Word that removes obstacles and hindrances from our lives!

WHEN WE SPEAK GOD'S WORD INTO A SITUATION IN OUR LIVES, AND COME AGAINST THE ENEMIES OF OUR SOUL, WE ARE CAUSING ANGELS TO GO TO WORK ON OUR BEHALF, HEARKENING TO THE VOICE OF HIS WORD!

Ps. 103:20
Bless the LORD, ye his angels that excel in strength, that do his commandments, hearkening unto the voice of his word.

We are His body, His arms, His legs, His hands, His feet, His mouth, His voice in the earth!

1 Cor. 12:20-21
But now are they many members, yet but one body, and the eye cannot say unto the hand, I have no need of thee: nor again the head to the feet, I have no need of you...
We are the voice of His Word in the earth!

Dan. 10:11-13
11   And he said unto me, O Daniel, a man greatly beloved, understand the words that I speak unto thee, and stand upright: for unto thee am I now sent. And when he had spoken this word unto me, I stood trembling.
12   Then said he unto me, Fear not, Daniel: for from the first day that thou didst set thine heart to understand and to chasten thyself before thy God, thy words were heard, and **I am come for thy words,**
13   But the prince of the kingdom of Persia withstood me one and twenty days: but, lo, Michael, one of the chief princes, came to help me;

The angel Gabrielle appeared unto Daniel and explained that the warring angels (mighty ones) had been engaged in a spiritual battle over the words that were spoken in prayer by Daniel.
Words have power when spoken into being...as you can see, there was a battle raging in the heavenlies over words.

Prov. 18:21
Death and life are in the power of the tongue.

Prov. 6:2
Thou art snared with the words of thy mouth; thou art taken with the words of thy mouth.

Eccl. 8:4
Where the word of a king is, there is power.

Rev. 1:5-6

5   And from Jesus Christ, who is the faithful witness, and the first begotten of the dead, and the prince of the kings of the earth. Unto him that loved us, and washed us from our sins in his own blood,

6   **And hath made us kings and priests unto God** and his Father; to him be glory and dominion forever and ever. Amen.

God's Word is powerful, and when God's Word is spoken by a born again, Holy Ghost filled, tongue talking believer, the kingdom of darkness is shaken to its very foundation.
Why do you think the enemy of your soul tries to stop you before you start? The devil is a deceiver, and is afraid of you when you know how to do battle with him. When we speak God's Word, God watches over it to bring it to pass!

Eccl. 8:4
Where the word of a king is, there is power.

Isa. 55:9-11

9   For as the heavens are higher than the earth, so are my ways higher than your ways, and my thoughts than your thoughts.

10   For as the rain cometh down, and the snow from heaven, and returneth not thither, but watereth the earth, and maketh it bring forth and bud, that it may give seed to the sower, and bread to the eater:

11   So shall my word be that goeth forth out of my mouth: it shall not return unto me void, but it shall accomplish that which I please, and it shall prosper in the thing whereto I sent it.

When we speak God's Word, we are causing the "mighty ones" to go to war on our behalf!

Joel 3:9-11

9   Proclaim ye this among the Gentiles **(non-Jews);** Prepare war, wake up the mighty men, let all the men of war draw near **(to the voice of God)**; let them come up **(into the throne room).**

10   Beat your plowshares into swords **(sword of the Spirit),** and your pruning hooks into spears **(intercession):** let the weak say **(speak the word),** I am strong **(in the Spirit)**

11   Assemble yourselves, and come, all ye heathen **(Gentiles),** and gather yourselves together round about: thither cause **thy mighty ones (warring angels) to come down (to the earth), O LORD!**

About now, the devil is telling you, (thoughts, and fiery darts)...**what a bunch of rubbish. Remember, the devil is a deceiver and has been around a long, long time, and is a supernatural, angelic being that hates anything or anyone that serves Our Lord Jesus Christ!**
Let's ask the Lord to open your eyes to the spiritual realm, aren't we also the Lord's servants?
II Ki. 6:15-18

15   And when the servant of the man of God was risen early, and gone forth, behold, an host compassed the city both with horses and chariots. And his servant said unto him, alas, my master! What shall we do?

16 And he answered, Fear not: for they that be with us are more than they that be with them.

17 And Elisha prayed, and said, LORD, I pray thee, open his eyes, that he may see And the LORD opened the eyes of the young man; and he saw: and, **behold, the mountain was full of horses and chariots of fire round about Elisha (warring angels).**

18 And when they came down to him, Elisha prayed unto the LORD, and said, Smite this people, I pray thee, with blindness. And he smote them with blindness **according to the word of Elisha.**

The warring angels go to war with the enemy of our soul the moment we utter the Word of God, as we wield the sword of the Spirit, according to the voice of His word!! Glory to God Almighty! Fear not, for they that be with us are more than they that be with them.

Ps. 29:1
Give unto the LORD, O ye mighty, (warring angels) give unto the LORD glory and strength.

Ps 149:5-9
5 Let the saints be joyful in glory: let them sing aloud upon their beds
6 Let the high praises of God be in their mouth, and a two-edged sword in their hand;
7 To execute vengeance upon the heathen, and punishments upon the people;
8 To bind their kings with chains, and their nobles with fetters of iron;
9 To execute upon them the judgment written: this honor have all his saints.

Ps. 118:8-11
8 It is better to trust in the LORD than to put confidence in princes
9 All nations compassed me about: but in the name of the LORD will I destroy them.
10 They compassed me about; yea, they compassed me about:
11 but in the name of the LORD I will destroy them.

Luke 10:19
Behold, I give unto you **power to tread on serpents and scorpions, and over all the power of the enemy: and nothing shall by any means hurt you.**

Eph. 6:12-18
12 For we wrestle not against flesh and blood, but against principalities, against powers, against the rulers of the darkness of this world, against spiritual wickedness in high places.
13 Wherefore take unto you **the whole armor of God that** ye may be able to withstand in the evil day, and having done all, to stand.
14 Stand therefore, having your loins girt about with truth, and having on the breastplate of righteousness;
15 And your feet shod with the preparation of the gospel of peace;
16 Above all, taking the shield of faith, wherewith ye shall be able to quench all the fiery darts of the wicked.
17 And take the helmet of salvation, and the sword of the Spirit, which is the word of God:
18 Praying always with all prayer and supplication in the Spirit, and watching thereunto with all perseverance and supplication for all saints;

James 4:7

Submit yourselves therefore to God. (an act of our will) Resist the devil, (an act of our will) and he will flee from you.

Rom. 8:34-39

34   Who is he that condemneth? **It is Christ that died, yea rather, that is risen again, who is even at the right hand of God, who also maketh intercession for us.**

35   Who shall separate us from the love of Christ? Shall tribulation, or distress, or persecution, or famine, or nakedness, or peril, or sword?

36   As it is written, for thy sake we are killed all the day long; we are accounted as sheep for the slaughter.

37   **Nay, in all these things we are more than conquerors through him that loved us.**

38   For I am persuaded, that neither death, nor life, nor angels, nor principalities, nor powers, nor things present, nor things to come,

39   Nor height, nor depth, nor any other creature, shall be able to separate us from the love of God, which is in Christ Jesus our Lord.

The body of Christ has not realized or come to the revelation that every new born again believer **is a** NEW CREATURE **in Christ Jesus. The church needs to realize that this new creature that we have become is not only an act of faith, but also an act of our will.** The OLD MAN is dead! **The contract on our life is** *PAID IN FULL,* **bought back from the power of sin and death!**

Rev 1:18

I am he that liveth, and was dead; and, behold, I am alive for evermore, Amen; and have the keys of hell and of death.

That is a message from Satan's conqueror, OUR LORD JESUS CHRIST, the First Conqueror! Jesus is not tantalizing us, Jesus is not exaggerating...Jesus is the Word, the Word is truth, the truth is Jesus.
Jesus is telling us how it really is for the new creature in Christ Jesus, the new man.

2 Cor. 5:17
Therefore if any man be in Christ, he is a new creature: old things are passed away; behold all things are become new.

All things are become new; the new man is master over the enemy! The old man lives in the realm of the past, past fears, past doubts, past sins, past hurts, past addictions, past thoughts, past ways of the old man, past ways of the flesh. Don't you believe the Word of God? "Old things are past away, behold, all things are become new"! [If you allow the new man to be a new man!]
Why do so many of God's children live in the past life of the old man? Why do so many of God's children live in the soulish realm? Why do so many of God's children live in the flesh? Because many don't have the revelation that the life of the new man is not only by faith, but also an act of our will.
Now, I am not talking about being under law. I'm talking about using our God given free will to conquer the enemy of our soul, through the power of the Holy Ghost and wielding the sword of the Spirit!
Why do you think we have a free will? Because God does not make robots! That's why!

Jesus said, "It is finished", on the cross, and then gave the authority on this earth to the church, through the body of Christ, which is the body of believers.
Jesus conquered the enemy at the cross.
Satan's dominion over us has been broken, the enemy is eternally defeated, the enemy is eternally conquered, we have been delivered out of the authority of Satan by the new birth, and we have been translated into the Kingdom of light.

Col. 1:12-14
12 Giving thanks unto the Father, which hath (**past tense**), made us meet
13 (worthy) to be partakers of the inheritance of the saints in light:

14 Who hath (**past tense**) delivered us from the power of darkness, and hath (**past tense**) translated us into the kingdom of his dear Son:
15 In whom we have redemption through his blood, even the forgiveness of sins (**past tense**):

Matt. 28:18
And Jesus came and spake unto them, saying, all power **is given unto me in heaven and in earth".**

Jesus said all power is given unto Me in heaven and earth. Let's look at the power!

THE POWER OF THE NAME OF JESUS

John 14:13-14
13 And whatsoever ye shall ask in my name, that will I do, that the Father may be glorified in the Son,
14 If ye shall ask any thing in my name, I will do it.

Jesus gives us the power of attorney to use **HIS NAME.**   When we speak the Word of God, using the name of Jesus, we conquer the forces of the enemy of our soul. **"We are more than conquerors through Him that loved us." We walk out of the realm of the past into the realm of a conqueror!   The past is over.   This is a day of new beginnings.**

Rom. 8:11-15
11 But if the Spirit of him that raised up Jesus from the dead dwell in you, **he that raised up Christ from the dead shall also quicken your mortal bodies by his Spirit that dwelleth in you.**
12 Therefore, brethren, we are debtors, not to the flesh, to live after the flesh
13 For if ye live after the flesh, ye shall die: but if ye through the Spirit do mortify the deeds of the body, ye shall live. (An act of our will.)
14 For as many as are led by the Spirit of God, they are the sons of God
15 For ye have not received the spirit of bondage again to fear; but ye have received the Spirit of adoption, whereby we cry, Abba, Father.

The Holy Ghost raised Jesus Christ from the dead, and the Holy Ghost lives in us. What He did in the dead body of Jesus Christ, He can do in your life! With the Holy Ghost in you, speaking the Word of God, in the name of Jesus (in His place), makes you a master over the enemy of your soul.   Satan tries to imitate the Holy Ghost by trying to resurrect the old man!
Knowledge of the Word of God is essential to our growth as a child of God. It is impossible for a believer to grow spiritually and remain uneducated in God's Word.

Being uneducated in the Word of God keeps the believer in bondage. The believer is actually taken captive and devastated by the enemy; neither realizing what belongs to them in Christ Jesus, nor understanding exactly what happened at the cross.

When Jesus said, "It is finished", He meant just that!

Spiritual growth occurs when we HAVE the revelation of the cross!

Many Christians are destroyed, or are still walking in bondage, because they have never been taught truth concerning who they are in Christ Jesus. But also how to walk in the victory that Jesus has already paid such a price for on the cross!

Isa. 5:13

Therefore my people are gone into captivity, because they have no knowledge: and their honorable men are famished, and their multitude dried up with thirst.

God wants us to walk in the fullness of what he has already provided, the power of the blood! (What the CROSS and the BLOOD of JESUS freely has given to the believer.) Glory to God!

SALVATION...Being born again, saved from eternal death and separation from God.

John 3:3

Jesus answered and said unto him, Verily, verily, I say unto thee, Except a man be born again, he cannot see the kingdom of God.

Acts 4:12

Neither is there salvation in any other: for there is none other name under heaven given among men, whereby we must be saved.

REDEMPTION...The contract on our life is paid for in full, bought back from the power of sin and death.

Eph. 1:7

In whom we have redemption through his blood, **the forgiveness of sins, according to the riches of his grace;**

Rev. 5:9

Thou art worthy to take the book, and to open the seals thereof: for thou wast slain, and hast redeemed us to God by thy blood **out of every kindred, and tongue, and people, and nation;**

ATONEMENT...The act by which God restores a relationship of harmony and unity between Himself and human beings.

Rom. 5:11

but we also joy in God through our Lord Jesus Christ, by whom we have now received the atonement.

RIGHTEOUSNESS...The Cross of Jesus is a public demonstration of God's righteousness. God accounts, or transfers, the righteousness of Christ to those who trust in Him. We do not become righteous because of our inherent goodness; God sees us as righteous because of our identification by faith with His Son.

2 Cor. 5:21
For he hath made him to be sin for us, who knew no sin; that we might be made the righteousness of God in him.

Rom. 3:25
Whom God hath set forth to be a propitiation through faith in his blood, to declare his righteousness for the remission of sins that are past, through the forbearance of God.

SANCTIFICATION... The process of God's grace by which the believer is separated from sin and becomes dedicated to God's righteousness, sanctification results in holiness, or purification from the guilt and power of sin.

Heb. 10:10
By which will we are sanctified through the offering of the body of Jesus Christ once for all.

Heb. 10:14
For by one offering he hath perfected forever them that are sanctified.

JUSTIFICATION... When God justifies, He charges the sin of man to Christ, and credits the righteousness of Christ to the believer (2 Cor. 5:21). Thus, "through one Man's righteous act, the free gift came to all men, resulting in justification of life."

Rom. 5:9
Much more then, being now justified by his blood, we shall be saved from wrath through him.

RECONCILED... The initiative in reconciliation was taken by God-- while we were still sinners and "enemies", Christ died for us. (Rom 5:8,10; Col. 1:21) Reconciliation is thus God's own completed act, something that takes place before human actions such as confession, repentance, and restitution. God, Himself, "has reconciled us to Himself through Jesus Christ". (2 Cor. 5:18)

Rom. 5:10
For if, when we were enemies, we were reconciled to God by the death of his Son, much more, being reconciled, we shall be saved by his life.

FORGIVENESS... The act of excusing or pardoning another, in spite of his slights, shortcomings, and errors. As a theological term, forgiveness refers to God's pardon of the sins of human beings.

Col. 2:13-14
13 And you, being dead in your sins and the uncircumcision of your flesh, hath he quickened together with him, having forgiven you all trespasses;
14 Blotting out the handwriting of ordinances that was against us, which was contrary to us, and took it out of the way, nailing it to his cross;

DELIVERED... The act of being delivered from the power of darkness, set at liberty from captivity.

Col. 1:13
Who hath delivered us from the power of darkness, and hath translated us into the kingdom of his dear Son:

OVERCOMING POWER... That which we receive, when we act upon what has been delegated to us.

Luke 10:19
Behold, I give unto you power to tread on serpents and scorpions, and over all the power of the enemy: and nothing shall by any means hurt you.
Rev. 12:11
And they overcame him by the blood of the Lamb, and by the word of their testimony; and they loved not their lives unto the death.
Eph. 2:6
And hath raised us up together, and made us sit together in heavenly places in Christ Jesus:

We have been set free, healed, and delivered! Now is the time to walk in the "Promised land." Don't stay in the wilderness forty years walking in circles. When Moses led the children of God out of Egypt into the desert to go to the "Promised land," it took them forty years to travel an eleven day journey! Why? They were listening to the thoughts and fiery darts of the enemy and were murmuring those thoughts and fiery darts from the enemy's camp. They were listening to their flesh and what their flesh wanted to do. The same thing the enemy does to us to get us to murmur to get us out of fellowship with God. Then the enemy can accuse us day and night before our Father!
We must have the revelation of what Satan is doing to us through thoughts and fiery darts, by an act of our own will.
If we don't recognize the enemy and put him in his place, by wielding the sword of the Spirit, we will be in the wilderness for forty years trying to make an eleven-day journey!

Exod. 16:2-3
2   And the whole congregation of the children of Israel murmured against Moses and Aaron in the wilderness:
3   And the children of Israel said unto them, Oh, that we had died by the hand of the LORD in the land of Egypt, when we sat by the flesh pots, and when we did eat bread to the full; for ye have brought us forth into this wilderness, to kill this whole assembly with hunger

1 Cor. 10:5-13
5   But with many of them God was not well pleased: for they were overthrown in the wilderness.
6   Now these things were our examples, to the intent we should not lust after evil things, as they also lusted.
7   Neither be ye idolaters, as were some of them; as it is written, the people sat down to eat and drink, and rose up to play.
8   Neither let us commit fornication, as some of them committed, and fell in one day three and twenty thousand.
9   Neither let us tempt Christ, as some of them also tempted, and were destroyed of \serpents.

10 Neither murmur ye, as some of them also murmured, and were destroyed of the destroyer.
11 Now all these things happened unto them for ensamples: and they are written for our admonition, upon whom the ends of the world are come.
12 Therefore let him who thinks he stands take heed lest he fall.
13 There hath no temptation taken you but such as is common to man: but God is faithful, who will not suffer you to be tempted above that ye are able; but will with the temptation also make a way to escape, that ye may be able to bear it.

In order to possess the Promised Land, we have to believe, receive, and act upon God's Word that God's will may be done in the earth, and in our lives. That is the Kingdom of God.

Matt. 6:10
Thy kingdom come Thy will be done in earth, as it is in heaven.

Eph. 1:3
Blessed be the God and Father of our Lord Jesus Christ, who hath blessed us with all spiritual blessings in heavenly places in Christ.

Notice that God has blessed us with every spiritual blessing. We are blessed because we are in the Promised Land. We are enriched with every blessing.
The problem is that the devil has kept us in the wilderness through a lack of knowledge, and our own passivity. The word "passivity" simply means a lack of activity, no self-control, or inaction.
God wants us to willfully cooperate with Him. We must actively choose God, daily, minute by minute, hour by hour, by an act of our own free will. When we do, freedom of the spirit comes.
When we don't cooperate with God, evil spirits take advantage of our inactive state to accomplish their wiles (strategy).
Only the powers of darkness want us to be inactive in regards to spiritual things, not God.
Before we were born again, we were enslaved to Satan, and therefore, not free. But after the new birth, we are free to choose what is from God. However, we must make a choice of *whom to serve*. Satan never wants to let go of us, so he continually devises ways to try to recapture us. Normally, it is the same way he caught us before being born again.
Remember, after the new birth, Satan has no rights to us anymore, so he can only deceive us and try to recapture our will.
Because of our free will, neither God nor the devil can do anything without our consent. We must decide for ourselves whom we will serve, daily.

Duet. 30:19
I call heaven and earth to record this day against you, that I have set before you life and death, blessing and cursing: therefore choose life, that both thou and thy seed may live.

God calls us to choose, willingly, to do His will so that our spirit, soul, and body may be free. God asks us to work with Him. Satan deceives man to be his slave and captive. Satan forces man to be his puppet...to be passive so his evil spirits can operate in our lives.

Rom. 6:16

Know ye not, that to whom ye yield yourselves servants to obey, his servants ye are to whom ye obey; whether of sin unto death, or of obedience unto righteousness?

Many of God's children wonder why God does not protect us from the onslaught of the enemy. I have told many that because God has given us a free will, that there are various conditions set down by God that we must fulfill, to be protected from evil spirits. If we have not exercised our authority in the spiritual realm, we are open to the enemy. We must recognize the strongholds in our life. We must recognize the wills of the flesh. We must realize those that are deceived have good intentions. You can be honest as the day is long and doing your best in life, but if you don't have the correct knowledge of the spiritual realm, know your authority, know who you are in Christ, and aren't humble enough to acknowledge the possibility of being deceived, you will be.

It is difficult for the Holy Ghost to teach you if your *mind is closed.*

The enemy has managed to overcome many believers because of not being teachable!

God calls us to obey Him and to resist Satan...AN ACT OF OUR FREE WILL.

James 4:7

Submit yourselves (your flesh) therefore to God. Resist the devil, and he will flee from you.

Submit yourselves (pray in the Spirit) to God. Resist the devil, (wield the sword of the Spirit), and he will flee from you. Prayer in the spirit enables us to inwardly overcome the enemy and also to deal with him. Prayer in the Spirit overcomes the flesh, building up our spirit.

Jude 1:20

But ye, beloved, building up yourselves on your most holy faith, praying in the Holy Ghost.

Rom. 8:26-27

26 Likewise the Spirit also helpeth our infirmities for we know not what we should pray for as we ought: but the Spirit itself maketh intercession for us with groanings which cannot be uttered.

27 And he that searcheth the hearts knoweth what is the mind of the Spirit, because he maketh intercession for the saints according to the will of God.

Many times we don't know what to pray for, but the Spirit of God knows our situation, as He searches our hearts to make intercession for us, according to God's will for our lives. Thank you Jesus. This is why we must submit ourselves to praying in the Spirit to God.

When we pray in the Spirit, we are able to overcome our flesh. As we pray in the Spirit, the fruits of the flesh begin to fall away, being replaced by the fruits of the Spirit. We have the authority to go after, and to get, the enemy out of our lives.

God exhorts us to resist the devil. God will not resist for us: we must do so, ourselves.

We must resist the thoughts and the temptations of sinful flesh. We must resist the wills of the flesh. We must resist the evil that is around us, daily. Our free will, and the Holy Ghost, chases the enemy away.

We must realize we have spiritual authority to remove the enemy.

We must pray daily, as prayer enables us to inwardly overcome the enemy, then to outwardly deal with him. We must read and meditate in god's word daily. The kingdom of God is within you. Kingdom authority.

Reread and meditate on this document until you fully understand the entire content before moving on to document #6.

If you are having a problem understanding the content, pray and ask the Holy Spirit to enlighten the eyes of your understanding.

WATCHMAN RON

Two thousand years ago a decree was issued from the judgment seat of God. The judgment provides protection for the Church against the onslaught of Satan and his evil spirits.

When Jesus died on the cross for us who were yet sinners, the ruler of this world was judged. Our debts were nailed to the cross of Jesus Christ and cancelled, *paid in full*. Principalities and powers were disarmed. Because of the work on the cross by Jesus, we have a blood covenant not only to be protected from our enemy, but also to triumph over him. The Blood of Jesus Christ was so complete, and the judicial decision from God against Satan that we have divine protection. The Blood of Jesus Christ has truly set us free from the law of sin and death. The word of God is the eternal sword to reinforce the victory through the Blood of Jesus Christ.

The Word of God is the eternal sword to reinforce the victory through the Blood of Jesus Christ. We have the authority to destroy the strongholds that the enemy is resurrecting in the old man.

We have the authority to overcome the wills of the flesh. All we have to do is to give our free will to the Holy Ghost and allow him to go to war with the enemy of our soul. Allowing the Holy Ghost to overcome sin, flesh, and the devil; this is an act of our will, and *not* by "faith".

The cross of Jesus did it all. The Holy Spirit administers what was accomplished, the cross gives us position, and obedience to the Holy Ghost makes us a spiritual reality, able to walk in spiritual power.

The only thing that can hinder us from the fullness of what God has for us in this life and the future is our own flesh. Therefore, if you recognize strongholds and wills of the flesh in your life, you will be able to make significant progress. The more you recognize and overcome your flesh, the more spiritual you will become. Unless you are willing to deal with your flesh, your growth will be shallow.

We must learn to overcome the old man, denying and resisting the power of the flesh in all things. Prayer is the acid test of your spirit man.

A strong spirit is capable of praying much with perseverance to overcome strongholds and wills of the flesh.

The entrance to the spiritual realm through the in filling of the Holy Spirit is our invitation to overcome. Let us go on unto perfection.

Most Christians pray for what we already possess through Jesus.

Example:
Isa. 53:4-5

4   4   Surely he hath borne our griefs, and carried our sorrows: yet we did   esteem him stricken, smitten of God, and afflicted

5   But he was wounded for our transgressions, he was bruised for our iniquities: the chastisement of our peace was upon him; and with his stripes we are healed.

Not "maybe", not "will be"...we are healed, set free, and delivered! We already possess it!

I hear people say, "If only I had faith". My dear people, it is not a faith problem!

It's a fact that we are not walking in the Promised Land. Come on over to the Promised Land. You have been set free, healed, and delivered. The enemy has already been defeated. Come out of the wilderness where you have been walking in circles. Walk in the promises of God, walk in the Kingdom of God!

Heb. 6:1-2

1   Therefore leaving the principles of the doctrine of Christ, **let us go on unto perfection;** not laying again the foundation of repentance from dead works, and of faith toward God,

2   Of the doctrine of baptisms, and of laying on of hands, and of resurrection of the dead, and of eternal judgment.

We are to go on unto perfection. In other words, get off of the milk. We are to speak the word of God into our situations.

Matt. 8:7-13

7   And Jesus saith unto him, I will come and heal him.

8   The centurion answered and said, Lord, I am not worthy that thou shouldest come under my roof: **but speak the word only, and my servant shall be healed.**

9   **For I am a man under authority,** having soldiers under me: and I say to this man, Go, and he goeth; and to another, Come, and he cometh; and to my servant, Do this, and he doeth it.

10   When Jesus heard it, he marveled, and said to them that followed, Verily I say unto you, I have not found so great faith, no, not in Israel.

11   And I say unto you, that many shall come from the east and west, and shall sit down with Abraham, and Isaac, and Jacob, in the kingdom of heaven.

12   But the children of the kingdom shall be cast out into outer darkness: there shall be weeping and gnashing of teeth.

13   And Jesus said unto the centurion, Go thy way; and as thou hast believed, so be it done unto thee. **And his servant was healed in the self same hour.**

When we walk in kingdom authority, we only have to speak the word for God to move on our behalf.
The Apostle Paul prays for the saints at Ephesus, and to the faithful in Christ Jesus.

Eph. 1:17-23

17   That the God of our Lord Jesus Christ, the Father of glory, may give unto you the spirit of wisdom and revelation in the knowledge of him:

18   **The eyes of your understanding being enlightened;** that ye may know what is the hope of his calling, and what the riches of the glory of his inheritance in the saints,

19   And what is the exceeding greatness of his power to us-ward who believe, according to the working of his mighty power, (the same Holy Ghost power is in us!)

20   Which he wrought in Christ, when he raised him from the dead, and set him at his own right hand in the heavenly places, (we are seated in heavenly places with Him).

21   Far above all principality, and power, and might, and dominion, and every name that is named, not only in this world, but also in that which is to come:

22   And hath put all things under his feet, and gave him to be the head over all things to the church,

23   Which is his body, the fullness of him that filleth all in all.

The victory of our Lord Jesus Christ placed believers far above the powers of Satan and his angelic hosts of fallen angels.

I Jn. 4:4
Ye are of God, little children, and have overcome them: because greater is he that is in you, than he that is in the world.

Eph. 6:11
Put on the whole armor of God that ye may be able to stand against the wiles of the devil. (An act of our will.)

Our Lord Jesus Christ tells us in:
Matt. 10:27-28, 34
27 What I tell you in darkness, that speak ye in light: and what ye hear in the ear, that preach ye upon the housetops
28 And fear not them which kill the body, but are not able to kill the soul: **but rather fear him which is able to destroy both soul and body in hell.**
34 **Think not that I am come to send peace on earth:** I came not to send peace, but a sword.

John 10:10
The thief cometh not, but for to steal, and to kill, and to destroy: **I am come that they might have life and that they might have it more abundantly.**

Satan will give you the kingdoms of this world, if you will serve him!
Satan offered the kingdoms of this world to Jesus.

Matt. 4:8-9
8 Again, the devil taketh him up into an exceeding high mountain, and sheweth him all the kingdoms of the world, and the glory of them;
9 And saith unto him, all these things will I give thee, if thou wilt fall down and worship me.

It is written in the Word of God that Satan is full of wisdom, as he was created that way in the beginning. When God created him as the anointed cherub angel that covereth, in the beginning, he was a beautiful creation of God.

Ezek. 28:13-19
13 Thou hast been in Eden the garden of God; every precious stone was thy covering, the sardius, topaz, and the diamond, the beryl, the onyx, and the jasper, the sapphire, the emerald, and the carbuncle, and gold: the workmanship of thy tabrets and of thy pipes was prepared in thee in the day that thou wast created.
14 Thou art the anointed cherub that covereth; and I have set thee so: thou wast upon the holy mountain of God; thou hast walked up and down in the midst of the stones of fire.
15 Thou wast perfect in thy ways from the day that thou wast created, till iniquity was found in thee.
16 By the multitude of thy merchandise they have filled the midst of thee with violence, and thou hast sinned: therefore I will cast thee as profane out of the mountain of God: and I will destroy thee, O covering cherub, from the midst of the stones of fire.
17 Thine heart was lifted up because of thy beauty, thou hast corrupted thy wisdom by reason of thy brightness: I will cast thee to the ground, I will lay thee before kings, that they may behold thee.
18 Thou hast defiled thy sanctuaries by the multitude of thine iniquities, by the iniquity of thy traffick; therefore will I bring forth a fire from the midst of thee, it shall devour thee, and I will bring thee to ashes upon the earth in the sight of all them that behold thee

19   All they that know thee among the people shall be astonished at thee: thou shalt be a terror, and never shalt thou be any more.

Satan is not omnipresent. Only God is able to be present in all places, at the same time. The only way that Satan can operate is through his hierarchy of fallen angels.

Eph. 6:12
For we wrestle not against flesh and blood, but against principalities, against powers, against the rulers of the darkness of this world, against spiritual wickedness in high places.
He is also god of this world system.

2 Cor. 4:4
In whom the god of this world **hath blinded the minds of them which believe not, lest the light of the glorious gospel of Christ, who is the image of God, should shine unto them.**

He is also the "prince of the power of the air".

Eph. 2:2-3
2   Wherein in time past ye walked according to the course of this world, according to the **prince of the power of the air,** the spirit that now worketh in the children of disobedience:
3   Among whom also we all had our conversation in times past in the lusts of our flesh, fulfilling the desires of the flesh and of the mind; and were by nature the children of wrath.

Jesus called him "the prince of this world".

John 12:31
Now is the judgment of this world: now shall *the prince of this world* **be cast out.**
Satan must rely on his demonic hosts, (fallen angels), in diversified places to administer his power, as he is not all knowing or able to be in all places at all times. This explains why Christians are not fighting against flesh and blood (people), but against spiritual wickedness in high places.

Rev. 12:7
And there was war in heaven: Michael and his angels fought against the dragon; and the dragon fought and his angels.

There was a war in the heavenlies between Michael and his angels and the dragon (Satan) and his angels. Michael is the commander in chief of heaven's armies, and throughout the Bible is the Great Prince that stands up for Israel.

Rev. 12:8
And prevailed not; neither was their place found any more in heaven.

Satan prevailed not (Satan and his host lost the battle in the heavenlies). Satan was cast out of the *THIRD HEAVEN* (where God is) with one third of the angels, those that rebelled against God. ANGELS ALSO HAVE A FREE WILL! Satan has been in the *heavens one and two* (the atmosphere and stratosphere) since his fall, that is why he is called "prince of the air". Satan will remain there until he is cast to the

earth during the last half of the tribulation hour, when he will possess the body of the anti-christ.

Rev. 12:9
And the great dragon was cast out, that old serpent called the Devil, and Satan, which deceiveth the whole world: he was cast out into the earth, and his angels were cast out with him.

Let me briefly explain the three heavens to you as it will help you to understand how Satan and his hosts operate against you, and also where Satan and his hosts belong at this time, according to the Word of God.
As you will see when we do battle with Satan and his hosts, it is important to send him back to where he belongs, as they are not in the "wilderness" or in the "pit", as of yet, as God has an appointed time for dealing with Satan and his host.   Satan knows he has to deal with God at an appointed time, that's why he doesn't worry about God, at this time.   The Church of Jesus Christ (you and me) are his enemy. The world already serves him.
The Word of God plainly shows us that there are three heavens the first heaven is the home of the birds and the clouds.

The first heaven...

Ps. 104:12
By them shall the fowls of the heaven have their habitation, which sing among the branches.

Ezek. 31:6
All the fowls of heaven made their nests in his boughs.

Ezek. 29:5
I have given thee for meat to the beasts of the field and to the fowls of the heaven.

It can be seen that as beautiful as this heaven of birds and clouds can be, it is not the eternal home of the redeemed.

The second heaven ...Home of the sun, moon, and stars.

Gen. 1:8
And God called the firmament Heaven.

Gen. 1:16-17
16 And God made two great lights; the greater light to rule the day, (the sun) and the lesser light to rule the night: (the moon) he made the stars also.
17 And God set them (the sun and the moon) in **the firmament of the heaven** to give light upon the earth...

Ps. 19:1
The heavens declare the glory of God; and the firmament sheweth his handiwork.

The firmament is the visible arch of the sky, the home of the sun, moon, and stars. America landed on the moon in 1969, and has succeeded in developing a spacecraft to transport man from the first heaven into the second heaven! But as wonderful as it is, the second heaven, just like the first heaven, cannot be confused with the heaven of salvation!

The third heaven...The home of God!

2 Cor. 12:2 (Paul the Apostle)
I knew a man in Christ above fourteen years ago, (whether in the body, I cannot tell; or whether out of the body, I cannot tell: God knoweth;) such a one caught up to the third heaven.

I King 8:27
But will God indeed dwell on the earth? Behold, the heaven and heaven of heavens **cannot contain thee; how much less this house that I have built?**

According to the book of Job, Satan goes to and fro in the earth, and walks up and down in it. He is headquartered in the first and second heavens.

Luke 21:25-27 (Jesus speaking of the last days)
25 And there shall be signs in the sun, and in the moon, and in the stars; and upon the earth distress of nations, with perplexity; the sea and the waves roaring;
26 Men's hearts failing them for fear, and for looking after those things which are coming on the earth: **for the powers of heaven shall be shaken.** (Satan's dwelling place!)
27 And then shall they see the Son of man coming in a cloud with power and great glory.

Matt. 6:9 (Jesus teaches us how to pray)
After this manner therefore pray ye: **Our Father which art in heaven,** hallowed be Thy Name.

Jesus is referring to the Third Heaven, the abode of Almighty God!!
Satan was cast out of the third heaven in Isa.14:12-14.

Isa. 14:12-14
12 How art thou fallen from heaven, O Lucifer, son of the morning! How art thou cut down to the ground, which didst weaken the nations!
13 For thou hast said in thine heart, I will ascend into heaven; I will exalt my throne above the stars of God: I will sit also upon the mount of the congregation, in the sides of the north:
14 I will ascend above the heights of the clouds; **I will be like the most High.**

Satan was cast out of the third heaven for rebellion against God.
Satan will be cast out of the first and second heavens in Rev. 12:9.

Rev. 12:9
And the great dragon was cast out, that old serpent, called the Devil, and Satan, which deceiveth the whole world: he was cast out into the earth, and his angels were cast out with him. Satan will be cast into the lake of fire in Rev. 20:10.

Rev. 20:10

And the devil that deceived them was cast into the lake of fire and brimstone, where the beast and the false prophet are, and shall be tormented day and night forever and ever.

Rev. 12:10-11
10   And I heard a loud voice saying in heaven, now is come salvation, and strength, and the kingdom of our God, and the power of his Christ: **for the accuser of our brethren is cast down, which accused them before our God day and night.**
11   And they overcame him by the blood of the Lamb and by the word of their testimony; and they loved not their lives unto the death.

Please notice that in Rev. 12:10 that Satan was accusing the brethren before God day and night.   He can only accuse us if we have given him the ground to do so.   In other words, we have allowed Satan to ascend over us by an act of our will, either by passivity, or by not casting down those thoughts and fiery darts and taking them captive to the Word of God.

How did the saints in Rev. 12:11 overcome the devil?

Rev. 12:11
And they overcame him by the blood of the Lamb, and by the word of their testimony; and they loved not their lives unto the death.

They overcome Satan by the Blood of the Lamb (they were set free, healed, and delivered at the cross) and by the word ("logos, the written word!) of their testimony (evidence given, witness, record)...It is written!!
How do we overcome the devil? WE SPEAK THE WORD ONLY!
We speak the written Word of God, which is the written record that enforces the victory over him by the Blood of the Lamb at the Cross, at the Resurrection, at the Ascension, and by maintaining our seat in heavenly places with Christ Jesus!
What is the written record to speak over our own life, our spouse, our children, our families, our ministry, our home, our church, our health, our finances, and all the provision that God has provided for us through His beloved Son, Our Lord and Savior Jesus Christ?
What is the written record to overcome the onslaughts of the deceiver, and liar Satan and all of his host?
What written record spoken by you, by an act of your will, will keep the enemy at bay, and under your feet?
The *written record* **is about what has already set us free from Satan and his hosts!**
The *written record* **about the BLOOD OF THE LAMB!**
We overcame him Satan and his hosts, principalities, powers, rulers of the darkness of this world, and spiritual wickedness in high places By the Blood of the Lamb!

Eph. 6:12
For we wrestle not against flesh and blood, but against principalities, against powers, against the rulers of the darkness of this world, against spiritual wickedness in high places.

Rev. 12:11
And they overcame him by the blood of the Lamb, and by the word of their testimony; and they loved not their lives unto the death.

Rom. 5:9
Much more then, being now justified by his blood, we shall be saved from wrath through him.

Col. 1:20
And, having made peace through the blood of His cross, by Him to reconcile all things unto Himself; by Him, I say, whether they be things in earth, or things in heaven.

Eph. 1:7
In whom we have redemption through His blood, the forgiveness of sins, according to the riches of His grace.

Rom 5:9
Much more then, being now justified by His blood, we shall be saved from wrath through Him.

Heb. 13:12
Wherefore Jesus also, that He might sanctify the people with His own blood, suffered without the gate.

I Jn. 1:7
But if we walk in the light, as he is in the light, we have fellowship one with another, and the blood of Jesus Christ his Son cleanseth us from all sin.
Lev. 17:11
For the life of the flesh is in the blood: and I have given it to you upon the altar to make an atonement for your souls: for it is the blood that maketh an atonement for the soul.

Heb. 9:22
And almost all things are by the law purged with blood; and without shedding of blood is no remission [of sin].

Col. 1:13-14
13 Who hath delivered us from the power of darkness, and hath translated us into the kingdom of His dear Son:
14 In whom we have redemption through His blood, even the forgiveness of sins:

Rev. 5:9
And they sung a new song, saying, Thou art worthy to take the book, and to open the seals thereof: for Thou wast slain, and hast redeemed us to God by thy blood out of every kindred, and tongue, and people, and nation.

Heb. 9:12
But by His own blood, He entered in once into the holy place, having obtained eternal redemption for us.

Heb. 9:14
How much more shall the blood of Christ, who through the eternal Spirit offered himself without spot to God, purge your conscience from dead works to serve the living God?

Heb. 10:19
Having therefore, brethren, boldness to enter into the holiest by the blood of Jesus.

Rev. 19:13
And he was clothed with vesture dipped in blood: and His name is called The Word of God.

Rev. 12:11
And they overcame him by the blood of the Lamb, **and by the** word of their testimony; **and they loved not their lives unto the death.**

The enemy has been defeated! Satan was defeated at the cross 2000 years ago. BY THE BLOOD, BY THE BLOOD, BY THE BLOOD. he is a defeated foe, a "has-been"! The *enemy* **is our spiritual enemy, our mental enemy, our emotional enemy, our physical enemy, and our financial enemy.**
Satan will try to operate through anything, or anyone, to try to defeat us. He will use the vehicle of STRONGHOLDS of past sin, past addictions, past temptations that he has used before. Doubt and unbelief, condemnation, fear, anger, self-pity, oppression, depression, lust, greed, insecurity, discouragement, sickness and disease, bitterness, criticism, murder, rape, theft, lies...just to name a few.
Check your spirit man; you may be surprised at what the enemy has been doing in your mind...the battleground of your soul!
Most believers don't realize they have authority in the spirit realm, or how to use it. We received spiritual authority when we were born again and filled with the Holy Ghost. We are new creatures in Christ Jesus, the old man died at the cross!

Phil. 2:5
Let this mind be in you, which was also in Christ Jesus.

Phil. 2:8-15
8   and being found in fashion as a man, He humbled himself, and became obedient unto death, even the death of the cross.
9   Wherefore God also hath highly exalted Him, and given Him a name **which is above every name**:
10   That at the name of Jesus, every knee should bow, of things in heaven, and things in earth, and things under the earth;
11   and that every tongue should confess that Jesus Christ is Lord, to the glory of God the Father.
12   Wherefore, my beloved, as ye have always obeyed, not as in my presence only, but now much more in my absence, **work out your own salvation with fear and trembling**
13   For it is God which worketh in you both to will and to do of his good pleasure
14   Do all things without murmurings and disputings:
15   **That ye may be blameless and harmless, the sons of God**, without rebuke, in the midst of a crooked and perverse nation, among whom ye shine as lights in the world;

Phil. 2:20-21
20   For I have no man like-minded,
21   For all seek their own, not the things which are Jesus Christ's.

We are to be likeminded, to think and have the mind of Christ, to be blameless and harmless, the sons of God.

I Jn. 4:17

Herein is our love made perfect, that we may have boldness in the Day of Judgment: **because as He is, so are we in this world.**

1 Cor. 2:16
For who hath known the mind of the Lord, that He may instruct him?
But we have the mind of Christ.

We, the Church, are His body, His hands, His feet, His mouth, His voice in the earth; we are the body of Christ, to do as He would do in the earth. IN HIS NAME, in other words...IN HIS PLACE! When we use the name of Jesus, it is as though Jesus Himself were doing the speaking. The enemy responds as it would respond to Jesus. JESUS GAVE US AUTHORITY TO DO SO!

Acts 3:2-8
2   And a certain man lame from his mother's womb was carried, whom they laid daily at the gate of the temple which is called Beautiful, to ask alms of them that entered into the temple;
3   Who seeing Peter and John about to go into the temple asked an alms.
4   And Peter, fastening his eyes upon him with John, said, look on us,
5   and he gave heed unto them, expecting to receive something of them.
6   Then Peter said, silver and gold have I none; but such as I have give I thee: In the name of Jesus Christ of Nazareth rise up and walk!
7   And he took him by the right hand, and lifted him up: and immediately his feet and ankle bones received strength,
8   and he, leaping up, stood, and walked, and entered with them into the temple, walking, and leaping, and praising God.

As a believer speaks the word of God in name of Jesus, it avails with our Father, and tears down strongholds of the enemy. The enemy of our soul doesn't want us to learn how to use this authority...Kingdom authority! Speak the word only, in the name of Jesus.

WE ARE HIS VOICE IN THE EARTH.
WE ARE THE SONS OF GOD.
THE ENEMY WANTS TO DECEIVE YOU!
THE ENEMY WANTS TO DISARM YOU!
THE ENEMY WANTS TO DEFEAT YOU!
THE ENEMY WANTS TO OVERCOME YOU!

2 Pet. 2:19
For of whom a man is overcome, of the same is he brought in bondage.
The very first step to freedom is to know the truth of all things: truth concerning cooperation with God, the operation of evil spirits, and supernatural manifestations. We, as the children of God, must know the truth as to the source and nature of the experiences we may encounter while we are overcoming.

Step by step, we ascend to freedom. Our free will must rise up to oppose the rule of evil spirits: To recover all lost ground. To work actively with God for the pulling down of strongholds.

I personally have experienced several encounters with evil spirits while coming against the enemy of my soul. And having experienced these manifestations in my flesh and body, it is only fair to warn you, not of any danger, but to expect temptations of the flesh to increase. These temptations can be so intense that you will think it is a manifestation of your stronghold.

During this period of time when we begin to overcome, the enemy and the flesh are in a very intense struggle with our free will and the Holy Ghost. Because of the resistance of the enemy, you will find that in the beginning stages of battle, the temptations and stimulation of the flesh will be stronger than before. THE DEVIL IS TRYING TO STOP YOU BEFORE YOU START.

The more you come against the enemy, the more he will begin to weaken. This phenomenon is the beginning signs of your FREEDOM. This experience is demonstrating to you that you are having an effect on the enemy, and that the enemy is feeling the pressure that his stronghold is not wanted, and that you have the revelation of his deception.

When we patiently and methodically take back our ground, little by little, we are restored.

Remember not to stop the battle until full freedom is restored. You will know when you are free.

When the enemy has us trapped in a stronghold that has taken him years to put in place, and then deceived us for even more years, even after we were born again, that enemy does not want to give you up.

When we are bound, we are doing Satan's bidding...sinning against a Holy God.

The work of the Holy Ghost is to bring the Christian into perfect obedience of self-control, by an act of our OWN free will. (Gal. 5:22-23)

We are in a spiritual battle. As a believer, we must have the revelation that the power of God is backing us, that the enemy was defeated at the cross, and that the old man is dead.

We cannot defeat the enemy by faith alone! We defeat the enemy by wielding the sword of the Spirit, and having on all of our armor. Faith alone can make us passive. The faith message has helped many of us to understand God's faith and how to believe His word and His promises for our lives. However, the faith message has also made some believers passive in their spiritual struggle. The believer is still trying to "believe" God for what Jesus has already paid for, in full, on the cross.

Because they are trying to "believe" God for their healing or deliverance, or some other problem in their lives, they become passive and exert no action in the spiritual realm. Because of this deception by the enemy, we are overcome by the enemy and are still held in bondage. Being passive in our spiritual life is extremely dangerous!

Passivity is one of the most effective weapons Satan has. Satan can overcome us and bring us into bondage, even when we are believing God in the situation. If we don't get free from the problem, we will eventually become frustrated and blame God Himself for our problem.

God has already made provision for any situation in our lives caused by the enemy, through His Son Jesus Christ. That's what Jesus meant when He said, "IT IS FINISHED!"

When you have revelation, and you recognize the battle you are in, you will have no problem facing the enemy. In other words, we are the enforcers of God's will upon the earth.

Matt. 6:10
Thy kingdom come Thy will be done in earth, **as it is in heaven.**

Example: Today's Policeman.

When the policeman puts on his uniform, badge and gun, he represents authority in the natural realm, and is responsible to enforce the law and fights against evil in our towns, cities, and nation and even within families, (domestic violence). The authority is given to him by the local, state, or national government, and stands behind him.

We are to put on the full armor of God and enforce God's will upon the earth in our towns, our cities, our nation, our families and strongholds within ourselves.

God fights the battle through His heavenly hosts, and enforces His word when we speak "it is written" standing behind us as we enforce the written record.

Rom. 13:11-14

11 **And that, knowing the time, that now it is high time to awake out of sleep: for now is our salvation nearer than when we believed.**

12 The night is far spent, the day is at hand: let us therefore cast off the works of darkness, and let us **put on the armor of light.**

13 Let us walk honestly, as in the day; not in rioting and drunkenness, not in chambering and wantonness, not in strife and envying

14 But put ye on the Lord Jesus Christ, and make not provision for the flesh, to fulfill the lusts thereof

Eph. 4:22-27

22 That ye put off concerning the former conversation the old man, which is corrupt according to the deceitful lusts;

23 And be renewed in the spirit of your mind;

24 And that ye **put on the new man,** which after God is created in righteousness and true holiness.

25 Wherefore putting away lying, speak every man truth with his neighbor: for we are members one of another.

26 Be ye angry, and sin not: let not the sun go down upon your   wrath:

27 Neither give place to the devil.

Eph. 6:11-12

11 Put on the whole armor of God, that ye may be able to stand against the wiles of the devil

12 For we wrestle not against flesh and blood, but against principalities, against powers, against the rulers of the darkness of this world, against spiritual wickedness in high places.

Col. 3:12

Put on therefore, as the elect of God, **holy and beloved, bowels of mercies, kindness, humbleness of mind, meekness, longsuffering.**

We are to put on, as the elect of God, all of the armor **that God has provided for us and go on to perfection.   Putting on the armor of light and the Lord Jesus Christ, and make no provision for the flesh.   Putting off the old man, not giving place to the devil!**

The Lord is behind us to back us whenever we are battling the enemy.

Like the policeman is just an ordinary man, until he "puts on'" his uniform, badge and gun, (which represents his authority to enforce the law), with the local, state, or federal government backing him! The policeman is fighting a battle in the natural realm against evil.

WE ARE CALLED TO FIGHT THE BATTLE IN THE SPIRITUAL REALM!

FATHER,
I WILL NOT BE PASSIVE.
I WILL CAST DOWN VAIN IMAGINATIONS.
I WILL NOT LISTEN TO THE CONVERSATIONS OF THE ENEMY ANY LONGER.
THE OLD MAN IS DEAD.
I WILL REFUSE THE ENTRY OF THE ENEMY.
I WILL RESIST THE ENEMIES FUTHER WORKINGS.
I RESOLVE, CHOOSE, AND REFUSE TO BE CONTROLED BY STONGHOLDS OF THE FLESH.
I WILL NOT FOLLOW STRONGHOLDS BLINDLY.
I INTEND TO BE MY OWN MASTER.
I RESOLVE TO CONTROL MYSELF.
I KNOW WHAT TO DO.
I WILL SPEAK THE WORD ONLY.
I WILL NOT CONSENT TO THE MANIPULATION OF MY FLESH.
I BIND THE SPIRIT OF BONDAGE AND LOOSE THE SPIRIT OF FREEDOM.
THE PAST IS OVER; THIS IS A DAY OF NEW BEGINNINGS.
THE KINGDOM OF GOD IS WITHIN ME.
I AM A NEW MAN A NEW CREATURE THROUGH CHRIST JESUS.
I AM MORE THAN A CONQUEROR THROUGH CHRIST JESUS.
THANK YOU JESUS FOR GOING TO THE CROSS FOR ME.
THANK YOU JESUS FOR SHEDDING YOUR BLOOD FOR ME.
THANK YOU JESUS FOR SETTING ME FREE FROM THE POWER OF SIN AND DEATH.

For it is written:
Rev. 12:11
And they overcame him by the blood of the Lamb and by the word of their testimony; and they loved not their lives unto the death.

We are to lay hands on the sick not the old man. You were delivered at the cross-by the blood of the lamb. We teach you how to overcome strongholds from your past and wills of the flesh.
The Word of God teaches that we must overcome sin, flesh and the devil by an act of our own free will. In other words submit to God (the Holy Spirit) an act of our free will by praying in the spirit.
Resist the devil by casting down vain imaginations, thoughts, fiery darts, and wielding the sword of the spirit, and praying in tongues. (An act of our free will.)
The word of God teaches us to lay hands on the sick, to impart gifts, to fill with the holy spirit or when the church sets someone apart for a special task such as the mission field, a pastorate, etc.;

HANDS, LAYING ON OF

On the DAY OF ATONEMENT, the priest laid his hands on the SCAPEGOAT (Lev. 16:12). This symbolized the transferal of the sins and guilt of the people to the

goat The act of laying on of hands in the Old Testament was also associated with blessing (Gen. 48:18), installation to office (Deut. 34:9), and the setting apart of Levi (Num. 8:10). Expressing the idea of transferal of authority and quality.

In the New Testament Jesus laid his hands on children (Matt. 19:13,15) and on the sick when he healed them (Matt. 9:18). In the early church the laying on of hands was also associated with healing, the reception of the Holy Spirit (Acts 9:17), the setting apart of persons to particular offices and work in the church (Acts 6:6), the commissioning of Barnabas and Paul as missionaries (Acts 13:3), and the setting apart of Timothy (1 Tim. 4:14; 2 Tim. 1:6). It expressed the idea of being set apart by the entire church for a special task.

(from Nelson's Illustrated Bible Dictionary)
(Copyright (C) 1986, Thomas Nelson Publishers)

We are to go on unto perfection.

Heb 6:1-2
1   Therefore leaving the principles of the doctrine of Christ, let us go
        on unto perfection; not laying again the foundation of repentance from dead
        works, and of faith toward God,
2   Of the doctrine of baptisms, and of laying on of hands, and of
        resurrection of the dead, and of eternal judgment.

This is why Jesus is telling us to hear what the spirit is saying to the churches in the book of revelation chapters 2 & 3 when he is speaking to the New Testament church about being an overcomer.   We are to overcome sin, flesh and the devil.

How do we overcome the evil spirit that comes against us using vehicles of strongholds and the wills of our flesh?   WE SPEAK THE WORD ONLY, WIELDING THE SWORD OF THE SPIRIT, AND PRAY IN THE SPIRIT.

We speak the written Word of God, which is the written record that enforces the victory over evil spirits by the blood of the lamb at the cross, at the resurrection, at the ascension, and by maintaining our seat in heavenly places with Christ Jesus!

What is the written record to speak over our own life, our spouse, our children, our families, our ministry, our home, our church, our health, our finances, and all the provision that God has provided for us through His beloved Son, Our Lord and Savior Jesus Christ?

What are the written record to overcome the onslaughts of the deceiver, and liar Satan and his host?

What written record spoken by you, by an act of your will, will keep the enemy at bay and under your feet?

The written record about what has already set us free, from Satan and his hosts!

The written record about the BLOOD OF THE LAMB!

We overcame Satan and his hosts, principalities, powers, rulers of the darkness of this world, and spiritual wickedness in high places By the Blood of the Lamb!

AFTER REPENTANCE:
WE LOOSE GOD'S WRITTEN WORD ABOUT THE BLOOD OF THE LAMB, AND PRAY IN TONGUES
WE THEN BEGIN TO OVERCOME THE THOUGHTS, TEMPTATIONS, AND WILLS OF THE FLESH.
WE ARE AT THIS POINT IN YOUR TRAINING UTILIZING EIGHT OF THE TEN KEYS GIVEN TO US BY THE HOLY SPIRIT

1	REPENTANCE
2	THE INFILLING OF THE HOLY SPIRIT
3	THE POWER OF TONGUES
4	THE POWER OF ANOINTED PRAYER (TONGUES)
5	THE POWER OF THE RESURECTION (REINFORCED)
6	THE POWER OF THE WORD OF GOD
7	THE NAME OF JESUS (IN HIS NAME, IN HIS PLACE)
8	THE POWER OF THE BLOOD................. (GOD'S WORD ABOUT THE BLOOD OF THE LAMB AND WHO YOU ARE IN CHRIST JESUS THROUGH THE BLOOD REINFORCED)

WINNING THE BATTLE IS NOT THE DIFFICULT PART!
IT IS RECOGNIZING THE BATTLE!
IT IS RECOGNIZING THE ENEMY!
IT IS RECOGNIZING THE STRONGHOLD!
IT IS RECOGNIZING YOUR FLESH!
IT IS RECOGNIZING YOUR WEAPONS!
IT IS RECOGNIZING WHO YOU ARE IN CHRIST!
WINNING THE BATTLE IS NOT THE DIFFICULT PART, FOR YOUR ENEMY IS A DEFEATED FOE.
THE DIFICULT PART IS RECOGNIZING THE THOUGHTS, THE FIERY DARTS, and THE WILLS OF THE FLESH.
WHEN WE SPEAK GOD'S WORD INTO A SITUATION IN OUR LIVES, AND COME AGAINST THE ENEMIES OF OUR SOUL.
WE ARE CAUSING ANGELS TO GO TO WORK ON OUR BEHALF HEARKENING TO THE VOICE OF HIS BLOOD!

Reread and meditate on this document until you fully understand the entire content before moving on to document #7.
If you are having a problem understanding the content, pray and ask the Holy Spirit to enlighten the eyes of your understanding.

WATCHMAN RON

The opening of the eyes of our understanding and the knowledge of the truth of God's word is God's word is absolutely necessary for deliverance from the deception of the enemy of our soul. Without the opening of the eyes of our understanding, freedom is impossible.

This ministry has attempted to destroy the walls of arguments, theories, and reasoning's, replacing the wall with the truth of God's word. We have also shown you how that by being passive in your Christian walk, and not exerting any action in the spiritual realm, you will be overcome by the enemy of your soul. Being passive is one of the most effective weapons that Satan has. Being passive in our spiritual live is extremely dangerous.

Satan can actually overcome us and bring us into bondage even when we believe God *by faith*, if we do not exert action in the spiritual realm.

Once you have discerned the deception of the enemy, and recognize the conversations of the enemy with the old man and your flesh, you are gaining ground on the enemy. Deception unlatches the gate for evil spirits to come in, and passivity provides a place for them to stay. The combination of deception and passivity will equal entrenchment. Spiritual warfare is necessary when a Christian is entrenched by the enemy.

The common factor is the inactivity of your free will. We, as Christians, must learn to obey God's will, to resist Satan's will, and exercise our own will in cooperation with God's will.

The work of the Holy Ghost is to bring our old man and our flesh into self-control.

When we pray in the Spirit, we are submitting our will to God's will for ourselves. The more we pray in the spirit, the quicker we begin to walk in the fruits of the spirit.

The fruits of the Spirit are:

Gal 5:22-25

22   But the fruit of the Spirit is love, joy, peace, longsuffering,
        gentleness,
        goodness, faith,

23   Meekness, temperance: against such there is no law

24   And they that are Christ's have crucified the flesh with the affections and lusts.

25   If we live in the Spirit, let us also walk in the Spirit.

The more we pray in the Spirit, the more quickly we come into self-control.

God expects us to be faithful. We must be strengthened by the Holy Spirit to even be able to obey God and be faithful.

God first works in us "to will", and then works in us "to work" for His good pleasure. (Phil 2:13)

We are called to fight the battle in the Spirit Realm!

II Ki. 6:15-17

15   And when the servant of the man of God was risen early and gone
        forth, behold, an host compassed the city both with horses and chariots. And his
        servant said unto him, alas, my master what
        shall we do?

16   And he answered, Fear not: for they that be with us are more than
        they that be with them.

And Elisha prayed, and said, LORD, I pray thee, open his eyes, that he may see. And the LORD opened the eyes of the young man; and he saw: and, behold, the mountain was full of horses and chariots of fire round about Elisha.

I Jn. 4:4

3   Ye are of God, little children, and have overcome them: because
        greater is He that is in you, than he that is in the world.

Winning the battle is not the difficult part; the enemy is a defeated foe! The enemy was defeated at the cross by the Blood of Jesus.
It is recognizing the battle, the thoughts, the fiery darts, the temptations, the old man, the flesh, the STRONGHOLD, and the ADDICTION.
It is recognizing your weapons and your armor, and wielding the sword of the Spirit, "it is written", by an act of your free will.
It is recognizing the enemy, and not being passive.
Satan is a deceiver, the father of all lies, he wants to deceive, disarm, defeat, and overcome you!
GREATER IS HE THAT BACKS US, THAN HE WHO BACKS THEM!
We are His body, His enforcers upon the earth; God wants us to exercise His will on the earth.
Jesus is not on the cross anymore, He is at the right hand of the Father.
The Church and the believer are the voice of His Word. God has delegated to us to carry on the work that Jesus began.
God is more concerned about our being faithful to what He has told us to do than He is in our doing *what we think we should be doing,* for Him.
When we stand before the Lord Jesus Christ at the judgment seat of Christ, who is the righteous judge, we will not be able to say, "Lord look at all I have done". Jesus will be asking us, "Did we do what He had told us to do?"
In other words, are you faithful?
Let me ask you right now, are you faithful to do what God has called you to do, or have you become passive in your spiritual walk? It is better to find out now before it is too late.

Luke 6:46
And why call ye me, Lord, Lord, and do not the things which I say?
According to the Apostle Paul, "the just shall live by faith."

Rom. 1:17
For therein is the righteousness of God revealed from faith to faith: as it is written, the just shall live by faith.
Romans 1:17 is a quote of Habakkuk 2:4, "but the just shall live by his faith". The original Hebrew word for faith is 'emuwnah (em-oo-naw'); KJV-- faith (-ful, -ly, -ness, stability, steady, truly, truth), this literally means "faithfulness" or "trustworthiness".

Most Christians would be surprised to learn that the English word "faith" appears only two times in the entire King James Version of the Old Testament. (Duet. 32:20 and Habak 2:4.) Both times it is used, it refers not to faith as we think of it, but "Faithfulness".

Many believers read Hebrews 11, which chronicles the exploits of the Old Testament saints. We have marveled at the great faith of these men of the Old Testament.

Heb. 11:7
By faith Noah, being warned of God of things not seen as yet, moved with fear, **prepared an ark to the saving of his house; by which he condemned the world, and became heir of the righteousness which is by faith.**
Although Noah moved with fear, he still moved. He was faithful.

Heb. 11:8
By faith Abraham, when he was called to go out into a place, which he should after receive for an inheritance, obeyed; and he went out, not knowing whither he went.
Abraham did not know where he was going. He was faithful.
Heb. 11:11
Through faith also Sara herself received strength to conceive seed, and was delivered of a child when she was past age, because she judged him faithful who had promised.

Sara was faithful in acting upon what God had told her. She was faithful.
In reality, what is being emphasized in these passages is not their great faith, but how they pleased God because of their great "faithfulness."
This is the reason many Christians grow weary of standing in "faith" during their trials. They are not standing to please God; they are standing to get a desired result.
While they are standing on God's Word, their eyes are on the manifestation of the answer of their need, rather than their "faithful" obedience to God's Word.
As a result, when the desired result does not manifest itself, in a week or two, they try a different approach. Usually in the natural realm, as they were trying to obtain a result that would spare them some trial.
The Church of Jesus Christ must come to the understanding that the word "faith" many times actually means "faithfulness".
The only reason to stand in "faith" is that by doing so we are being "faithful" to God and pleasing to Him.
GOD WANTS US TO BE FAITHFUL.

Matt. 25:21
21   His Lord said unto him, well done, thou good and faithful servant:
        thou hast been faithful over a few things, I will make thee ruler over many
        things: enter thou into the joy of thy lord.

God wants us to move on to perfection and be faithful.
It is time believers moved on to perfection, and on to the will of God for our lives.
God wants us to be spiritual men and women, faithful and not fleshy (carnal).

1 Cor. 3:1-3
1   And I, brethren could not speak unto you as unto **spiritual,** but as unto **carnal,**
        even as unto babes in Christ.
2   I have fed you with milk, and not with meat: for hitherto ye were not able to
        bear it, neither yet now are ye able.
3   For ye are yet carnal: for whereas there is among you envying, and strife, and
        divisions, are ye not carnal, and walk as men?

Christians today are in two classes of believers.

SPIRITUAL and FLESHY!

Those that are in the flesh cannot please God. (Rom. 8:8)
We, by an act of our own free, will must decide to follow the things of the spirit and not yield to the flesh, and all of the temptations around us.
When we are born again our flesh remains the same as a sinner.
Our flesh is not born again or changed instantly like our spiritual new birth.
We must learn how to overcome the flesh.

Gal. 5:16-17
16   This I say then, Walk in the Spirit, and ye shall not fulfill the lust of the flesh.
17   For the flesh lusteth against the Spirit, and the Spirit against the
        flesh: and these are contrary the one to the other: so that ye cannot
        do the things that ye would.

The desires of the flesh are against the Spirit, and the desires of the Spirit are against the flesh.
They are contrary to each other.

CONTRARY ...AGAINST EACH OTHER!

A. Verb. antikeimai ^480^, "to be contrary" (anti, "against," keimai, "to lie"), <Gal. 5:17; (From Vine's Expository Dictionary of Biblical Words) © Copyright 1985, Thomas Nelson Publishers).

When sin has gained control of your flesh, your flesh will oppose anything which may interfere with its comfort and self pleasure.
It is evident that a person belongs to the flesh if he continues to act like an unsaved man and sins often. The flesh wants to throw temper tantrums. The flesh has a will of its own. The flesh always has a self-interest, self-existence, self-glory, self-opinion, and self-centered motives. The flesh has a very strong will, all of its own.
You will begin to notice this when you begin to pray in the Spirit for any length of time. Your flesh will try to literally exert its will over you as you begin to break through the "Vail of Flesh".
As we pray in the Spirit, the flesh wants to stop you before you can break through the "Vail of Flesh". This is wrestling in the spirit.
This resistance stops after you have broken through the "Vail of Flesh".

Gal. 5:24-25
24   And they that are Christ's have crucified the flesh with the affections and lusts.
25   If we live in the Spirit, let us also walk in the Spirit.

We were delivered from the power of sin through the Cross of Jesus Christ. The Holy Ghost enables us to overcome the wills of the flesh. Our flesh wants to rule our lives, and so does the Spirit. The Spirit and the flesh are complete opposites.
When you enter into spiritual battle prior to overcoming, you will begin to notice, after a time of spiritual warfare, that housed within you are two persons. The person of the Holy Spirit and the person of the flesh. Each of these "persons" wants victory over your free will.

To serve God or to serve your flesh. Most Christians are fleshy and are governed by their flesh. It is a strategy of Satan to make you think it is too difficult to overcome your flesh. When you give your will to the Holy Ghost, THE HOLY GHOST OVERCOMES FOR YOU. ALL YOU HAVE TO DO IS ALLOW THE HOLY GHOST TO PRAY THROUGH YOU, FOLLOW GOD'S INSTRUCTIONS, AND BE FAITHFUL.

What are some of these works of the flesh we must overcome? The flesh has many ways of manifestations. As we cover some of these, you will begin to recognize works of the flesh that you probably thought were normal.

Growing up in a wicked world, we do not recognize these manifestations.

Gal. 5:19-21

19 Now the works of the flesh are manifest, which are these; adultery, fornication, uncleanness, lasciviousness,

ADULTRY, FORNICATION, AN UNCLEAN SPIRIT, LUSTFUL DESIRES, SEXUAL SIN, PORNOGRAPHY, SEXUAL ADDICTION, PERVERSION, HOMOSEXUALITY, LESBIANISM, SELF PLEASURE, THESE ARE ALL WORKS OF THE FLESH – ADDICTIONS OF THE FLESH.

20 Idolatry, witchcraft, hatred, variance, emulation's, wrath, strife, sedition's, heresies,

WORSHIPPING OTHER GODS, PRIDE, HATRED, TEMPER, ANGER, RAGE, VIOLENCE, STRIFE, SELFISHNESS, GREED, SELF-PITY, PREJUDICE, BITTERNESS, UNFORGIVENESS, QUARRELING, JEALOUSY, FURY, VENGEANCE, REVENGE, INDICTIVENESS, FIGHTING, DISCORD, REBELLION, RELIGION, WORKS OF THE FLESH

21 Envyings, murders, drunkenness, revellings, and such like of the which I tell you before, as I have also told you in time past, that they which do such things shall not inherit the kingdom of God.

ENVY, CRITICISM, MURDER, JUDGEMENT, OVERCOME BY ALCOHOL OR LOSING CONTROL OF ONES EMOTIONS, WORKS OF THE FLESH. IN ADDITION, THERE ARE WORKS OF THE ENEMY SUCH AS: OPPRESSION, DEPRESSION, ANXIETY, CONFUSION, DISTRESS, DISCOURAGEMENT, DOUBT, FEAR, GUILT, INSECURITY, INFERIORITY, LYING, NEGATIVENESS, PAST HURTS, POVERTY, REJECTION, SHAME, STRESS, THIEVERY, DOUBT, UNBELIEF, WORRY, SPIRITS OF INFIRMITY, SICKNESS and DISEASE.

These works of the flesh and works of the enemy cause much heartache.

Heartaches such as:
DIVORCE, MARITAL PROBLEMS, FAMILY PROBLEMS, WORK PLACE PROBLEMS, RELATIONSHIP PROBLEMS, DRUG and ALCOHOL ADDICTION, SEXUAL ADDICTION, SICKNESS AND DISEASE, FINANCIAL PROBLEMS...

It is time to go to war to get the enemy off your back! It is time to go to war to overcome the strongholds in your life that the enemy is using to destroy your home, your marriage, and your relationship with others. It is time to go to war so you can

have a fruitful relationship with the Lord Jesus Christ.

Gal. 5:22-25

22   But the fruit of the Spirit is love, joy, peace, longsuffering, g   gentleness, goodness, faith,

23   Meekness, temperance: against such there is no law.

24   And they that are Christ's have crucified the flesh with the affections and lusts.

25   If we live in the Spirit, let us also walk in the Spirit.

Our flesh was crucified with the Lord Jesus Christ, and the enemy is using strongholds of the mind and temptations of the flesh (that was crucified) to resurrect your past life.

REMEMBER: Satan has no power to resurrect anything. The enemy must tempt your flesh to get you to act on your own free will to sin.

The enemy must tempt your flesh to get you to react to his fiery darts of anger, temper, violence, or some other lust of the flesh.

When you go to war against the enemy of your soul, you will soon realize how deceived you have been. The minor works of the flesh will fall away as you pray in your spiritual language. You will begin to notice that as the minor works of the flesh fall away, they are replaced by the fruits of the Spirit. They are: love, joy, peace, longsuffering, gentleness, goodness, faith, meekness, and temperance, as you begin to walk in the Spirit.

The major works of the flesh that are left are the strongholds you will have to overcome using the instructions God has given to us according to His word. You will recognize the works of the enemy much more quickly and will be able to deal with them quickly. After you have learned how to recognize and how to overcome the works of the enemy, you will notice that they do not come around any longer! How sweet it is!

We have finally returned to normal. The conversations are gone, the temptations are gone, and the wills of the flesh are now under your control.

From here forward, it is a simple task of maintaining your prayer life and spending time with the Lord.

We keep our spirit sweet and soft by maintaining our prayer life and relationship with our Father, and the Lord Jesus Christ. FREEDOM OF SPIRIT IS OUR GOD GIVEN RIGHT, PAID FOR BY THE BLOOD OF THE LORD JESUS CHRIST.

Jesus dealt with the sin of our flesh on the cross. (Rom. 6:6) BY THE BLOOD--

Jesus delivered us from the power of sin so that sin may not reign again. BY THE BLOOD--

The Holy Ghost who dwells in the believer enables us to overcome the flesh daily to be able to obey the Lord.

When we are born again, our sins are forgiven. We are now a new man through Christ Jesus.

Once you realize who you are in Christ Jesus, and will allow the Holy Ghost to reveal to you how Jesus dealt with your flesh on the cross, you will possess and have the revelation of your victory.

When you proceed faithfully, without quitting or giving up, allowing the enemy to stop you before you start, you will overcome the flesh.

Always remember to disregard feelings of the flesh to be truly victorious in the spiritual realm.

Learn to always be aggressive towards the enemy of your soul.

Matt. 26:41

41   Watch and pray that ye enter not into temptation: the spirit indeed
        is willing, but the flesh is weak.

As long as we maintain our prayer life, we will have a fruitful life with our Lord. However, the presence of the flesh is always a call to watch and pray. Due to what Jesus did for us on the cross, and by being faithful in leaning upon the Holy Ghost, although the flesh still exists, you will find that the flesh loses all its resistance. Such a complete victory over flesh is attainable by all believers. I want to warn you to not become self-righteous in doing so. The flesh is flesh, good or bad. Because the flesh opposes the spirit, not only in sinning against God, but also the flesh will try to deceive you by leaning upon its own strength, rather than leaning upon God.

Remember, the flesh will even serve God if allowed to do so in its own strength.

This is one of the main reasons we must maintain our spiritual prayer life.

I cannot emphasize nor have the words to express the importance of maintaining spiritual prayer daily, in the Spirit. After prayer, you will literally "feel" the wall of protection placed around you by the Holy Ghost.

After you have overcome, it only takes an hour a day to maintain this hedge of protection, for not only you, but also your family and loved ones. How sweet it is! This is the duty of the Priesthood in the home.

Matt. 26:40-41

40   And he cometh unto the disciples, and findeth them asleep, and saith unto Peter, What, could ye not watch with me one hour?
41   Watch and pray that ye enter not into temptation: the spirit indeed is willing, but the flesh is weak.

Heb. 5:14
14   But strong meat belongeth to them that are of full age, even those who by reason of use have their senses exercised to discern both good and evil.

Heb. 6:1
Therefore leaving the principles of the doctrine of Christ, let us go on unto perfection.

WE HAVE A CHOICE TO SERVE GOD, AND NOT SERVE SIN, FLESH OR THE DEVIL. HOWEVER, WE MUST STILL MAKE THE CHOICE TO SERVE GOD! WE MUST USE THE POWER OF OUR FREE WILL DAILY!

Col. 3:5-10
5   Put to death, therefore, whatever belongs to your earthly nature: sexual immorality, impurity, lust, evil desires and greed, which is idolatry.
6   Because of these, the wrath of God is coming.
7   You used to walk in these ways, in the life you once lived.
8   But now you must rid yourselves of all such things as these: anger, rage, malice, slander, and filthy language from your lips.
9   Do not lie to each other, since you have taken off your old self with its practices
10   And have put on the new self, which is being renewed in knowledge in the image of its Creator. (NIV)

Eph. 6:13

Therefore, take up the full armor of God that you may be able to resist in the evil day, and having done everything, to stand firm.

Every time you see a "therefore" written, you should go back and see what it is "there for".
In this verse we see that the "therefore" is a reference to the nature of our struggle with principalities, powers, rulers of darkness, and spiritual wickedness, that is explained in verse 12.

Eph. 6:12

For we wrestle not against flesh and blood, but against principalities, against powers, against the rulers of the darkness of this world, against spiritual wickedness in high places.

This is also a repetition of the command in verse 11 to "put on the full armor of God." Anytime something is repeated like this in Scripture, we should understand it is because of the increased importance of what is being addressed.

Eph. 6:11

Put on the whole armor of God that ye may be able to stand against the wiles (strategies) of the devil.
If the word of God thought this was so important to repeat it so quickly, then we too should take the time to review the reason why.
Putting on the full armor of God is a crucial responsibility for every believer, yet there seems to be very little emphasis of this in most of the churches.
If we do not put on the armor of God, the enemy's strategies will get to us, our families and loved ones, and we will be repeatedly, and unnecessarily, wounded.
If we put on the full armor of God, the enemy is only wasting his efforts, since we will be protected. We are in a battle throughout our life on this earth.
Until the kingdom of God comes so that authority over the earth is restored to God, we are living in enemy territory.
If we do not put on the armor that God has provided for us in our mission here, we can expect continual harassment, which is precisely what many believers endure for their entire lives.
We have a choice. We have a free will.
What are you going to do about it?
Only the most foolish would not endeavor to learn how to put on the armor that has been provided for us.
The word of God repeats the words to "stand," as well as the word "firm."
For every soldier of the Lord Jesus Christ, we must have a commitment from the very beginning that we will never compromise our convictions, and we will never retreat from the enemies of our soul. We must stand firm regardless of the consequences. Retreat is not an option for us as the sons of God.
Every true believer should have a boldness and confidence, because we have the power and authority of the Holy Ghost.

We have a great advantage in this life—we can go to the end of the book and read the end of the story—we win! We have been promised success in this life, and a victory that will last forever!
How can we fail to be bold with such a promise from none other than God, Himself?

Those who are truly faithful will stand, and not compromise their convictions under any amount of pressure that the devil may bring.

The devil will test us, but those who really believe in the Lord Jesus Christ will always stand firm.

2 Pet. 1:4

Whereby are given unto us exceeding great and precious promises: that by these ye might be partakers of the divine nature, **having escaped the corruption that is in the world through lust.**

We have received God's divine nature, AND YET THE BIBLE MAKES IT CLEAR THAT A CHRISTIAN CAN SIN.

These are the words of a frustrated man, the Apostle Paul tells us in Romans chapter seven:

Rom. 7: 18-23

18   For I know that in me (**that is, in my flesh**) dwelleth no good thing: for to will is present with me; **but how to perform that which is good I find not**

19   For the good that I would I do not: but the evil which I would not, that I do

20   Now if I do that I would not, it is no more I that do it, but sin that dwelleth in me

21   I find then a law, that, when I would do good, evil is present with me

22   For I delight in the law of God after the inward man: (spirit man)

23   But I see another law in my members, warring against the law of my mind, (mind, will, emotions) and bringing me into captivity to the law of sin which is in my members (flesh)

This is exactly how Satan works against the believer...sound familiar?

Paul the Apostle is showing us how sin operates in our soul.

These are strongholds of the old man, the old sin nature, the flesh that was crucified with Christ on the cross.

Paul the Apostle was a man, just like us.

Satan is trying to continually resurrect the old man, so he can ascend over us to accuse us, day and night, before our heavenly Father. And in the process, strip us of our authority over him, taking us captive. Rebellion and self-centeredness are at the root of the old man, the old sin nature. These are thought patterns and behavior patterns of the old life, and until we overcome them with Holy Ghost prayer and the sword of the Spirit, we will continue to struggle. THERE IS NO OTHER WAY!

God has given us a free will to choose this day who we will serve.

Our Lord Jesus has paid the price for us, but through Him, we are the enforcers.

The strongholds that come against us are always habits or patterns of thought that were built-up in us while we were still servants of sin.

These thoughts have been in our lives for many years, and we have become so used to them that we think, behave, or feel (mind, will, emotions) that they are normal, and consequently we readily accept them as normal.

Eph. 4:22-24, 27

22   **That ye put off concerning the former conversation the old man, which is corrupt according to the deceitful lusts;**

23   And be renewed in the spirit of your mind;

24   **And that ye put on the new man,** which after God is created in righteousness and true holiness

If we continually fall, either in thought or in deed, to the same thought or behavior pattern repeatedly, then we have a stronghold in our lives, and the enemy is using the stronghold to keep us from being over comers.

Strongholds of the mind and addictions of the flesh are the enemy at work. They will kill, steal, and destroy everything that God has for us in this life, in our relationships with each other, our spouses, our families, our coworkers, and even Our Lord, ruining our witness of Jesus in our lives.

The enemy has a strategy for every one of us.

If we do not deal with the strongholds of the mind and addictions of the flesh, or if we will not deal with these through passivity, and we allow the enemy to continue to resurrect the old man, we will not have any joy in life on this earth. We will be a defeated Christian, running around from meeting to meeting trying to get deliverance from something we have already been delivered from at the cross. We will be too lazy to pick up the sword of the Spirit, and overcome the enemy.

If we do not, or will not, confront the strongholds and/or addictions in our lives, the enemy takes us captive and makes slaves out of us.

Strongholds of the mind and addictions of the flesh make us "prisoners in the Promised Land," "born again and bound," or "resurrected and not yet released."

There are characteristics of strongholds and addictions that, although they may differ from individual to individual, remain constant.

STRONGHOLDS and ADDICTIONS are stubborn, and if we try to overcome them in our own strength, we will fail and they will reappear.

Due to a lack of teaching in this area, most people give up and learn how to live with them!

I call it sleeping with the enemy!

Strongholds and addictions are strategies of Satan sent to destroy you!

Strongholds and addictions are remnants of the old man, the old sin nature! Strongholds are in the mind. Addictions are in the flesh. Thoughts and temptations are sent by Satan to entice you, to trap you, to sift you as wheat! Satan studies you and gives you what you want; he does not offer you what you do not want! Satan desires to have you! Strongholds and addictions drive us into traps of the enemy! Traps of the old man! Satan's kingdom is regimented; Satan's kingdom is organized to take you out of light into darkness! Strongholds and addictions are designed by Satan to take you back to the past, back to the traps of the old man! Satan has stolen our past; he is trying to steal the present through thoughts and fiery darts! Satan wants to steal our future, our eternal rewards for being an overcomer given out at the judgment seat of Christ!

The words of Jesus spoken to the church, to us:

Rev. 2:7
He that hath an ear let him hear what the spirit saith unto the churches; to him that overcometh will i give to eat of the tree of life, which is in the midst of the paradise of God.

Rev. 2:17
17   He that hath an ear, let him hear what the Spirit saith unto the churches; To him that overcometh will I give to eat of the hidden manna, and will give him a white stone, and in the stone a new name written, which no man knoweth saving he that receiveth it.

Rev. 2:26

26   And he that overcometh**, and keepeth my works unto the end, to him will I give power over the nations:**

Rev 3:21-22

21   **To him that overcometh** will I grant to sit with me in my throne, **even as I also overcame,** and am set down with my Father in his throne.

22   He that hath an ear let him hear what the Spirit saith unto the churches.

Rev. 21:7

7   **He that overcometh** shall inherit all things; and I will be his God, and he shall be my son.

We are called to overcome in this life! Today!
Overcome sin, flesh, and the devil!
Overcome strongholds and addictions!
Strongholds and addictions come in thoughts, temptations, fiery darts, and wills of the flesh, from the past life...the old man!

A stronghold is the vehicle used by evil spirits to override your free will:
Evil spirits using the vehicle of a stronghold to tempt your flesh to react to thoughts of:
Anger, anxiety, anorexia, bulimia, bitterness, condemnation, confusion, coveting, criticism, depression, discouragement, doubt, fear, greed, guilt, heartache, impatience, insecurity, judgmental, lust, lying, low self-esteem, materialism, mistrust, negative-ness, obesity, oppression, past hurts, poverty, pride, rebellion, rejection, religion, revenge, selfishness, self-pity, sexual addiction, self pleasure, shame, sickness, sin, sorrow, stress, strife, thievery, timidity, unbelief, un-forgiveness, violence, worry...strongholds have many names! The only authority they have is what we give them.
These strongholds belong to the old man. These problems of the flesh are strongholds of the enemy! Strongholds are always sent to kill, steal, and destroy what Jesus has already paid for.
John 10:10 the thief cometh not, but for to steal, to kill, and to destroy: I am come that they might have life, and that they might have it more abundantly.

Strongholds and addictions steal our abundant life! If we do not deal with our strongholds, If we do not recognize we have a problem, if we do not deal with the stronghold or addiction, we will not live the abundant life that Jesus has already paid for in full at the cross!
The old man died on the cross with Jesus Christ! The old man is dead! ...it is finished!
Satan wants to resurrect the old man through strongholds and addictions of the flesh. Satan wants to ascend over you to take your authority and dominion from you! Satan wants to accuse you day and night before your heavenly father!

2 Pet. 2:19
For of whom a man is overcome, of the same is he brought in bondage.

A stronghold or addiction is your deepest darkest secret! If you have a problem area in your life, you have a stronghold! Satan has a strategy for every one of us! Our father has a strategy for Satan and his demonic forces! A strategy to overcome the strongholds of the old man! A strategy to overcome sin, flesh, and the devil!

Eph. 4:11-13

11 and he gave some, apostles; and some, prophets; and some, evangelists; and some, pastors and teachers;

12 **For the perfecting of the saints**, for the work of the ministry, for the edifying of the body of Christ:

13 Till we all come in the unity of the faith, and of the knowledge of the Son of God, unto a perfect man, unto the measure of the stature of the fullness of Christ:

The knowledge in this guidebook is designed by God for the pulling down of strongholds and addictions! This is God's strategy to bring you to the place of perfection in him! It is time to leave the old and come into the new! It is time to leave the old man's ghost and learn how to overcome through the Holy Ghost!
Choose this day who you will serve. We are what we think about!
How can we bind the enemy if something is binding us?

2 Pet. 2:19
For of whom a man is overcome, of the same is he brought in bondage.

STRONGHOLDS AND ADDICTIONS are uncontrollable, if you have a habit or behavior pattern that seems to control you, you have discovered a stronghold or addiction that the enemy is using against you to strip you of your authority and your seat in heavenly places.
Remember, the enemy uses our mind, will, and emotions, (how we think, behave, or feel) to tempt us to fall and sin against a Holy God.

Luke 11:21-22

21   When a strong man armed keepeth his palace, his goods are in peace:

22   **But when a stronger than he shall come upon him, and overcome him**, he taketh from him all his armor wherein he trusted, and divideth his spoils.

2 Pet. 2:19
For of whom a man is overcome, of the same is he brought in bondage.

STRONGHOLDS cause us to act or react to negative situations in our lives that we have already been set free from at the cross of Our Lord Jesus Christ.
Remember that before we were born again, we were the victim of the perpetrator, so when the devil tries to remind you of your past, remind him of his future!
Because of Jesus, we have no past as we died at the cross with Him, Glory!

Rom. 6:6-7

6   **Knowing this, that our old man is crucified with him**, that the body of sin might be destroyed, that henceforth we should not serve sin

7   For he that is dead is freed from sin.

Jesus gave us the authority to do battle against the enemy and strongholds. We are the enforcers, the voice of His Word in the earth, The Voice of HIS Blood.

Evil spirits try to follow us around and try to take us captive through thoughts and fiery darts.

The biggest mistake the bride of Christ has made is not recognizing the enemy and not doing battle through passivity (no   action in the spirit realm).

If we could get rid of strongholds or addictions by faith, why do we have weapons of warfare?

How do Christians end up in a divorce?   Passivity...no action in the spirit realm!

How does an evil spirit pass from parent to child? Passivity...no action in the spirit realm!

Sad but true, the bride of Christ has been sleeping with the enemy, through passivity or a lack of knowledge.

We must come to the realization what the enemy is up to.

It is time to pick up the sword of the Spirit for not only ourselves, but also our brothers, sisters, and the leaders of the church, and their families.

The secular world and all their doctors are ineffective in trying to combat strongholds and addictions that have been put into place by the enemy.   All a doctor can do is to subdue them, sometimes, through medication.

We are in a spiritual battle, and only spiritual weapons will work. God has not left us defenseless against the forces of darkness.

For it is written:

Rev. 12:11
And they overcame him by the blood of the Lamb and by the word of their testimony; and they loved not their lives unto the death.

The opening of the eyes of our understanding and the knowledge of the truth of god's word is absolutely necessary for deliverance from the deception of the enemy of our soul. Without the opening of the eyes of our understanding freedom is impossible.

This ministry has attempted to destroy the walls of arguments, theories and reasoning, replacing the wall with the truth of God's word. We have also shown you how that by being passive in your Christian walk and not exerting any action in the spiritual realm you will be overcome by the enemy of your soul.

BEING PASSIVE IS ONE OF THE MOST EFFECTIVE WEAPONS THAT SATAN HAS.

Being passive in our spiritual life is extremely dangerous.

Satan can actually overcome us and bring us into bondage even when we are believing God by faith if we don't exert action in the spiritual realm. Once you have discerned the deception of the enemy, and recognize the conversations of the enemy with the old man and your flesh, you are gaining ground on the enemy. Deception unlatches the gate for evil spirits to come in; passivity provides a place for them to stay.

The combination of deception and passivity equals entrenchment.

Spiritual warfare is necessary when a Christian is entrenched by the enemy. The common factor is the inactivity of your free will.

We as Christians must learn to obey God's will, to resist Satan's will and exercise our own will in cooperation with God's will. The work of the Holy Ghost is to bring our old man and our flesh into self-control.

When we pray in the spirit we are submitting our will to God's will for our lives. The more we pray in the spirit, the quicker we BEGIN TO WALK IN THE FRUITS OF THE SPIRIT.

THE FRUITS OF THE SPIRIT ARE:

Gal 5:22-25
22   But the fruit of the Spirit is love, joy, peace, longsuffering, gentleness, goodness, faith,
23   Meekness, temperance: against such there is no law.
24   And they that are Christ's have crucified the flesh with the affections and lusts.
26   If we live in the Spirit, let us also walk in the Spirit.

The more we pray in the spirit the quicker we come into self-control.
God expects us to be faithful. We must be strengthened by the Holy Spirit to even be able to obey god and be faithful. God first works in us to will and then works in us to work his good pleasure. (Phil 2:13)

Reread and meditate on this document until you fully understand the entire content before moving on to document #8.

If you are having a problem understanding the content, pray and ask the Holy Spirit to enlighten the eyes of your understanding.

WATCHMAN RON

The opening of the eyes of our understanding and the knowledge of the truth of God's word is absolutely necessary for deliverance from the deception of the enemy of our soul. Without the opening of the eyes of our understanding, freedom is impossible.

The Voice of HIS Blood has attempted to destroy the walls of arguments, theories and reasoning, replacing the wall with the truth of God's word. We have also shown you how that by being passive in your Christian walk, and not exerting any action in the spiritual realm, you will be overcome by the enemy of your soul. Being passive is one of the most effective weapons that Satan has. Being passive in our spiritual life is extremely dangerous.

Satan can actually overcome us and bring us into bondage even when we believe God by faith, if we do not exert action in the spiritual realm.

Once you have discerned the deception of the enemy, and recognize the conversations of the enemy with the old man and your flesh, you are gaining ground on the enemy. Deception unlatches the gate for evil spirits to come in, passivity provides a place for them to stay.

The combination of deception and passivity equals entrenchment. Spiritual warfare is necessary when a Christian is entrenched by the enemy. The common factor for entrenchment is the inactivity of your own free will.

We as Christians must learn to obey God's will, to resist Satan's will, and exercise our own will in cooperation with God's will.

The work of the Holy Ghost is to bring our old man and our flesh into self-control. When we pray in the Spirit, we are submitting our will to God's will for our lives. The more we pray in the Spirit, the quicker we begin to walk in the fruits of the Spirit.

The fruits of the spirit are:
Gal 5:22-25

22   But the fruit of the Spirit is love, joy, peace, longsuffering,
        gentleness, goodness, faith,
23   Meekness, temperance: against such there is no law.
23   And they that are Christ's have crucified the flesh with the
        affections and lusts.
27   If we live in the Spirit, let us also walk in the Spirit.

The more we pray in the Spirit, the quicker we will come into self-control.

God expects us to be faithful. We must be strengthened by the Holy Spirit to even be able to obey God and be faithful.

God first works in us to will and then works in us to work his good pleasure. (Phil 2:13)

We as Christians in our ignorance have been deceived by the powers of darkness and have fulfilled the conditions for the enemy to work in our lives.

There are four steps the enemy lays down to trap us:
1. **Ignorance** – A lack of knowledge, education, or being unaware of the enemy at work in our lives
2. **Deception** – A deliberate act by the enemy to deprive us of our God given freedom paid for in full by the blood of Jesus Christ.
3   **Passivity** – inactivity on our behalf exerting no resistance in the spiritual realm against the enemy of our soul.

4   **Entrenchment** – the enemy has fortified his stronghold and taken the Christian captive by the combination of ignorance, deception, and our own passivity.

The eyes of our understanding have been opened to ignorance, deception, and passivity through the word of God. We are going to be teaching you how to overcome entrenchment of the soul. It is imperative that you follow the instructions we are teaching you. If you are not teachable, we cannot help you.

I want to point out that not everyone is entrenched by the enemy. Spiritual warfare for yourself is only necessary if you are entrenched, however, as a Christian, you still need to know how to do spiritual warfare in case the need arises. We as Christians can't be ignorant of the enemy's devices. *Remember that sickness and the enemy brings disease.*

You also need to know how to do spiritual warfare to overcome the spirit of infirmity. You may have a flesh problem to deal with, and the Holy Ghost will help you to overcome the flesh. All we have to do is submit to the Holy Ghost by praying in the Spirit for an hour daily. If an entrenchment is in place, it will surface repeatedly as you are praying in the spirit. At that time, you decide if you are entrenched by the enemy.

This entrenchment is the stronghold that is causing you to do the things you are doing that is contrary to the word of God. When you have a situation in your life that is controlling you and you are not able to stop or overcome it in the natural, you are entrenched.

This entrenchment can also be an addiction. An example would be the entrenchment of addiction of those who are caught up in pornography of some other sexual sin. This addiction actually causes the brain to release endogenous drugs or endogenous chemicals. Endogenous means "produced from within". Where cocaine or alcohol seek to mimic the brain's natural chemicals, pornography releases the real thing. This is today's new addiction.

Spiritual warfare is required to overcome this and several other entrenchment's.

It does not matter the depth of the entrenchment, as long as you decide daily to choose the will of God over your life and do it. This attitude will give God the opportunity to work his will in you and cause the influence of the evil spirit at work to weaken which in turn will strengthen you.

We must allow the Holy Spirit to rule over our renewed mind, will, and emotions. When we, as children of God, allow the flesh to rule, we will be rebellious to the things of god. When the Holy Spirit is allowed to rule, we produce spiritual fruit and the power of self-control.

Proverbs 25:28
28   He that hath no rule over his own spirit is like a city that is broken
      down, and without walls.

As you begin to pray, you may be surprised at what might surface because we as Christians tend to think that we are not bound in any area of our lives. God's truth is what sets us free. Satan's lies are what binds us. Continually pray that God will open the eyes of your understanding. Ask God to show you where you have been deceived. (Normally what you may fear to hear is most likely the ground you have given over to the enemy.)

You must realize that the choice is yours to make daily whom you will serve.

In spiritual warfare, we must decide to choose freedom and liberty and not be passive. We must speak God's Word over our lives while we are in warfare.

Having made the choice to overcome sin, flesh and the devil, reinforcing the Word of God, and utilizing our free will brings us closer to true freedom.

If you are entrenched, to resist in the beginning is truly a battle. This battle will require all the strength of the spirit, soul, and body. *This is wrestling in the spirit.*

Giving your free will to the Holy Ghost and speaking the Word of God over yourself will overcome the enemy and will chase him off of the stronghold that he is trying to protect. We must mobilize the Spiritual power that God has made available to us and drive out the enemy using the combination of all of the power keys to freedom that God has provided for us through the Blood of Jesus Christ.

1   The power of repentance
2   The power of the infilling of the Holy Ghost
3   The power of praying in the Spirit
4   The power of maintaining the fire of anointed Holy Ghost prayer
5   The power of the resurrection
6   The power of the Word of God
7   The power of the Name of Jesus
8   The power of the Blood
9   The power of praise and worship
10 The power of binding and loosing

The enemy must be driven out with Spiritual force. In taking back the ground that has been given over to the enemy, we must use all of these power gifts working together that God has provided for us. We must put on the full armor of God and resist the enemy and refuse giving him any more ground.

How do you do this? By rejecting the conversations of the enemy between the old man and your flesh that were previously accepted into your thought life and by *not acting or reacting* to the thought, fiery dart and temptation.

We must refuse to be manipulated by evil spirits that are using a stronghold to overcome us, and we must recognize when we are being enticed by the enemy and *not act on or react* to his enticement.

We must decide to recover all ground given to the enemy through ignorance, deception, or passivity. We must be faithful to follow God's instructions on overcoming the enemy of our soul. Do not believe the lies of the enemy any longer.

Withdraw from what you drew near to before that was able to entice you to return to sin, or react to the flesh.

In the beginning you will notice the resistance of the enemy trying to stop you before you start. This resistance will peak before it recedes and this in itself is a sign of victory that your resistance is having an effect. The enemy has felt the pressure and he will make his last stand. Keep the pressure on him and he will depart.

As long as you are faithful and continue to work to overcome these temporary attempts of the enemy trying to reinforce the stronghold, you will find yourself progressively being set free.

Our obedience to God is to be without question. God is the giver of all good gifts and of life itself, HE wants us to have life and to have it more abundantly.

It is the enemy who wants to kill, steal and destroy what God has done for us through his only begotten Son, Jesus Christ.

We must draw upon the power of the Holy Ghost, because it is impossible to stand-alone when we are dealing with supernatural, spiritual beings. God has given to us the Spiritual weapons and resources to overcome the enemy of our soul.

We are in a Spiritual battle, and this is why we need Spiritual weapons.

An *overcomer* is the Christian who has full authority to exercise his own will, is able to choose God's will, while rejecting Satan's will.

The work of the Holy Ghost within us is to bring our flesh and spirit-man into obedience to God's will for our lives. We are to be in control of our own lives by an act of our own free will. God wants us to be able to choose this day whom we want to serve, not being bound and controlled by evil spirits using a stronghold. God wants us to choose Him, by an act of our own choice. God wants us to be able to control our own mind, will and emotions.

The Voice of HIS Blood has taught you how to overcome temptations of the mind, will and emotions. We have taught you how to overcome strongholds and wills of the flesh. We have taught you how to recognize fortified walls that are called arguments, theories and reasoning (2 Corin. 10: 3-5). We have replaced those fortified walls with the truth of God's word.

The outer wall of pride will be replaced with a wall of humility as you begin to realize, and have the revelation, that we can do nothing without God.

We are now going to teach you how to overcome the enemy of your soul through Spiritual warfare, learning the power of binding and loosing' to overcome an entrenched evil spirit of bondage.

To overcome strongholds and addictions, to bind Satan, his principalities, powers and rulers of darkness, let us go on unto perfection. Winning the battle is not the difficult part; it is recognizing the enemy; it is recognizing the battle; it is recognizing your weapons; it is recognizing your flesh; it is putting on the full armor of god; it is acting upon your own free will to be an overcomer, and not be passive in your spiritual walk while on this earth.

THE POWER OF BINDING AND LOOSING

Matt. 16:13-19

13   When Jesus came into the coasts of Caesarea Philippi, he asked his disciples, saying, Whom do men say that I the Son of man am?

14   And they said, Some say that thou art John the Baptist: some, Elias; and others, Jeremias, or one of the prophets

15   He saith unto them, But whom say ye that I am?

16   And Simon Peter answered and said, Thou art the Christ, the Son of the living God.

17   And Jesus answered and said unto him, Blessed art thou, Simon Barjona: **for flesh and blood hath not revealed it unto thee, but my Father which is in heaven** (Revelation knowledge)

18   And I say also unto thee, That thou art Peter, and upon this rock I will build my church; and the gates of hell shall not prevail against it (Revelation knowledge)

19   And I will give unto thee (us) the keys (the Revelation knowledge) of the kingdom of heaven: (this is the Revelation) and whatsoever thou shalt bind on earth shall be bound in heaven: and whatsoever thou shalt loose on earth shall be loosed in heaven

Jesus is giving us, His church, the keys the revelation knowledge.
Jesus is telling us how the kingdom of heaven works (the first and second heavens.)
Where the hosts of Satan and his principalities, powers, and rulers of darkness are headquartered, and how to combat this kingdom by the power of binding and loosing, this is the rock that His church is to be built upon.

We have been given keys of the kingdom of heaven, Satan's kingdom.

Keys lock and unlock doors!   (bind= lock, loose = unlock.) We have the keys!

Matt. 18:18
Verily I say unto you, Whatsoever ye shall bind (lock) **on earth shall be bound** (locked) **in heaven: and whatsoever ye shall loose** (unlock) **on earth shall be loosed** (unlocked) **in heaven.**

God has given the body of Christ Spiritual weapons to come against the enemy of our soul.
The devil is a deceiver, he can only operate against us when we allow him to do so. However, the enemy is given much too much ground through a lack of teaching this truth, and passivity on the part of the believer.
It is sad but true, God's people are held captive in many ways to the enemy by deception, as he has been defeated and disarmed by Our Lord Jesus Christ at the cross.

Col. 2:15
And having spoiled principalities and powers, he made a shew of them openly, triumphing over them in it.

We have been given all of the armor and the revelation of how to combat an enemy, who is continually trying to resurrect the old man through deception.
We are a new man through Our Lord Christ Jesus!   Jesus has already paid the price!   It is up to us to enforce that defeat here on the earth.
We are the enforcers, God's policeman. We have been given the authority to bind the powers of darkness and loose the truth (the written record of God's Word). That is why Our Lord Jesus calls binding and loosing the "keys of the kingdom".
Keys lock and unlock doors to the realm of the supernatural.   The realm that controls our lives and how we cope in this life.   All evil can be bound in the Name of Jesus.
It is our use of the powers of God, delegated to us in the Name of Jesus, that overcome the strongholds of the enemy in our lives.
Whatever we bind, whatever we loose...keys of the kingdom.
Keys to become the overcomer that we have been called to be, in this life.   Keys to freedom from the strongholds and addictions of the enemy. Keys to freedom from the enemy's strongholds and addictions in our lives!

Rev. 3:12-13
Him that overcometh **will I make a pillar in the temple of my God, and he shall go no more out: and I will write upon him the name of my God, and the name of the city of my God, which is new Jerusalem, which cometh down out of heaven from my God: and I will write upon him my new name.**

When we use the weapons that God has given to us, we immediately begin to tear down the strongholds and addictions of the old man that the enemy of our soul has built around us, in the years before we were born again.
We tie up and stop the devil working in us (our mind, will, emotions) when we bind him and his evil kingdom from operating in our lives (our mind, will, emotions).
We must learn to be militant when it comes to binding the works of the enemy of our soul.
We must learn to war in the Spirit.   Why?

Eph. 6:12

For we wrestle not against flesh and blood, but against principalities, against powers, against the rulers of the darkness of this world, against spiritual wickedness in high places.

Remember that Satan has no power over us, as we were set free at the cross by the blood of the Lamb. Satan can only influence and tempt our mind, will, and emotions through thoughts and fiery darts. Satan must OVERCOME us to fall to his STRONGHOLD and ADDICTION.

If we don't take them captive according to God's Word, Satan tries to resurrect the old man, the stronghold or addiction.

Because the Holy Ghost lives in us, Satan has to leave and take his evil spirits with him when we OVERCOME him.

Rev. 12:11

And they overcame him by the blood of the Lamb, and by the word of their testimony; and they loved not their lives unto the death.

Ps. 34:7

The angel of the LORD encampeth round about them that fear him, and delivereth them.

Ps. 91:5

Thou shalt not be afraid for the terror by night; nor for the arrow that flieth by day.

Rom. 8:37

Nay, in all these things we are more than conquerors through him that loved us.

II Thes. 3:3

But the Lord is faithful, who shall stablish you, and keep you from evil.

Ps. 55:18

He hath delivered my soul in peace from the battle that was against me: for there were many with me.

Ps. 97:10

Ye that love the LORD, hate evil: he preserveth the souls of his saints; he delivereth them out of the hand of the wicked.

Ps. 107:2

Let the redeemed of the LORD say so, whom he hath redeemed from   the hand of the enemy;

I Jn. 4:4

Ye are of God, little children, and have overcome them: because greater is he that is in you, than he that is in the world.

Phil 4:13

I can do all things through Christ, which strengtheneth me.

Rev. 12:11

And they overcame him by the blood of the Lamb, and by the word of their testimony; and they loved not their lives unto the death.

BY THE BLOOD, BY THE BLOOD, OF THE LAMB!

No one can ever imagine how fully the soul of our Lord and Savior suffered on the cross. We often think about His suffering, but overlook the feelings of His soul.
A week before the Passover, He was heard to mention, "Now is my soul troubled." (John 12:27) This remark points to the cross.

John 12:27
Now is my soul troubled; and what shall I say? Father, save me from this hour: but for this cause came I unto this hour.

While in the garden of Gethsemane, the Lord Jesus was again heard saying, "My soul is very sorrowful even unto death."

Matt. 26:38
38   Then saith he unto them, My soul is exceeding sorrowful, even unto death: tarry ye here, and watch with me.

If it were it not for these words, we would not think His soul had suffered.
Isa. 53: 10-12 mentions three times how His soul was made an offering for sin.

Isa. 53:10-12
10   Yet it pleased the LORD to bruise him; he hath put him to grief: when thou shalt make his soul an offering for sin, he shall see his seed, he shall prolong his days, and the pleasure of the LORD shall prosper in his hand.
11   He shall see of the travail of his soul, and shall be satisfied: by his knowledge shall my righteous servant justify many; for he shall bear their iniquities.
12   Therefore will I divide him a portion with the great, and he shall divide the spoil with the strong; because he hath poured out his soul unto death: and he was numbered with the transgressors; and he bare the sin of many, and made intercession for the transgressors.

His soul travailed, and He poured out His soul to death.
Because Jesus bore the curse and shame of the cross, whoever believes in Jesus shall no more be cursed and put to shame.
Jesus was faithful and obedient all the way to the cross.
Jesus went to the cross by an act of His own free will so that you and I could be totally set free, healed, and delivered.

Luke 22:42
42   Saying, Father, if Thou be willing, remove this cup from Me: nevertheless not My will, but Thine, be done.

The Son of God was and is Holy, blameless, unstained, separated from sin.
He is united with the Holy Spirit in oneness.
Jesus cried out, "My God, My God, why hast thou forsaken me?" His soul felt loneliness, desertion, separation, from God. And yet, He was Faithful and Obedient all the way to the cross. Not for His own sake, but for the sake of you and me. Can we do any less for Him?

Eph. 6:12-18

12   For we wrestle not against flesh and blood, but against principalities, against powers, against the rulers of the darkness of this world, against spiritual wickedness in high places.

13   Wherefore take unto you the whole armor of God that ye may be able to withstand in the evil day, and having done all, to stand.

14   Stand therefore, having your loins girt about with truth, and having on the breastplate of righteousness;

15   And your feet shod with the preparation of the gospel of peace;

16   Above all, taking the shield of faith, wherewith ye shall be able to   quench all the fiery darts of the wicked.

17   And take the helmet of salvation, and the sword of the Spirit, which is the word of God:

18   Praying always with all prayer and supplication in the Spirit, and watching thereunto with all perseverance and supplication for all saints;

During a period of conflict, OUR WILL must be actively engaged in distinct operations.
Beyond choosing and Spiritual warfare, we must actively resist the temptations of the flesh, thoughts and fiery darts of evil spirits.
We must shut the door against the wiles of the enemy.
Shut the door on the temptations that open a door to a stronghold in you.
Example: Strongholds of Sexual Addiction

Satan tempts us with:
1   Thoughts of lust
2   Thoughts of past sin
3   Pornography
4   The opposite sex
5   Fantasies
6   Arousing your own bodies
7   X-rated movies
8   Television shows of nudity
9   Whatever triggers the addiction

To resist, in the beginning, is truly a battle. It requires all of the strength of the spirit, soul, and body.

The flesh is addicted to sensual pleasure. It is wrestling in the spirit.
We must mobilize all of our God given authority and Spiritual power, utilizing the Spiritual weapons that Jesus has given to us through the cross, removing the enemy of our soul.   When taking back the ground that the devil has stolen from us, we must resolve to fight, choose freedom, refuse ground, and resist the enemy. We must reclaim all ground until we arrive at the point of freedom we first enjoyed.
We should know from where we fell, and it is to that place we must be restored.
We need to understand what is normal for us.
In other words, our mind should be clear in not wanting to offend God any longer.
We start a new life following the recovery of this ground.
The past is over, and this day will be a day of new beginnings.
The thoughts are gone. The strongholds are gone. The addiction is gone.   The evil spirit is defeated. The devil is past tense…thank you Jesus!
We can all fall at any given time if we are not spiritually tuned in to the spiritual realm around us.
It is when we do not get back up and enter into the battle again that we lose the battle to the enemy of our soul.   Sad but true, most Christians today are to spiritually lazy and passive to press on to the mark of the high calling…it's easier to sleep with the enemy!
At some point, the enemy will mount their last struggle.   We must be strengthened through many battles.
We have enemies of depression, oppression, loneliness, rejection, anger, condemnation, fear, greed, insecurity, discouragement, sickness and disease, doubt and unbelief.
We have mental, emotional, and physical enemies. It is time that the church wakes up to the fact that Satan is on the loose looking for those he can devour.

1 Pet. 5:8

Be sober, be vigilant; **because your adversary the devil,** as a roaring lion, walketh about, seeking whom he may devour:

Acts 10:38

How God anointed Jesus of Nazareth with the Holy Ghost and with power: who went about doing good, and healing all that were oppressed of the devil; for God was with him.

As a believer, we are also anointed with the power of the Holy Ghost.

We can also go about doing good and healing those that are oppressed of the devil.

As we overcome the flesh, we begin walking in Kingdom Authority.

Jesus shows us by example, loosing' a woman from a spirit of infirmity.

Luke 13:12

And when Jesus saw her, He called her to Him, and said unto her, Woman, thou art loosed from thine infirmity.

Luke 13:13-15

13 And he laid his hands on her: and immediately she was made straight, and glorified God.

14 **And the ruler of the synagogue answered with indignation,** because that Jesus had healed on the Sabbath day, and said unto the people. There are six days in which men ought to work: in them therefore come and be healed, and not on the Sabbath day.

14 The Lord then answered him, and said, Thou hypocrite, doth not each one of you on the Sabbath loose his ox or his ass from the stall, and lead him away to watering?

Luke 13:16

Ought not this woman, being a daughter of Abraham, whom Satan hath bound, lo, these eighteen years, be loosed from this bond on the Sabbath day?

Notice...who bound this woman for eighteen years?

Wherever Our Lord Jesus went, He healed the sick. God was letting it be known that He wanted His people set free from oppression, sickness and disease.   Notice that in Luke 13:16 that Satan bound this woman for eighteen years, until Jesus came along and recognized the enemy!

You are learning how to recognize the enemy. The religious leaders of the day did not recognize that her problem was caused by Satan and his demonic hosts.

Religious leaders still do not recognize the enemy.

Mark 7:13

Making the word of God of none effect through your tradition.

Religious traditions make the Word of God ineffective; the devil uses religion to tey to void the Word of God.   Who do you think placed Jesus on the cross?

Religious traditions! Satan has many strategies.

We are to lay hands on the sick, loosing' them from a spirit of infirmity.

John 10:10

The thief cometh not, but for to steal, and to kill, and to destroy: I am come that they might have life and that they might have it more abundantly.

Jesus has said that He has come that we might have life, and that we might have it more abundantly.

God is not a thief, Jesus is not a thief, the Holy Ghost is not a thief! Wake up! Satan is the thief, sickness is the thief, oppression is the thief, depression is the thief, anger is the thief, fear is the thief, insecurity is the thief, discouragement is the thief, condemnation is the thief, disease is the thief, greed is the thief, divorce is the thief, criticism is the thief, judging is the thief, sexual addiction is the thief, anxiety is the thief, confusion is the thief, un-forgiveness is the thief, heartache is the thief, sin is the thief, self-pity is the thief, strongholds are a thief.

SATAN HAS MANY NAMES.

These, and many more thieves, come in the name of Satan!

We have an enemy seeking those whom he may devour! Satan and his hosts come to steal, kill, and destroy our life of abundance.

Jesus came that we might have life and have it more abundantly!

A life of abundance!

Acts 10:38

How God anointed Jesus of Nazareth with the Holy Ghost and with power: who went about doing good, and healing all that were oppressed of the devil...for God was with him.

And God is with us too! Glory be to God!

I Jn. 3:8

For this purpose the Son of God was manifested, that he might destroy the works of the devil.

Exod. 15:26

For I am the LORD that healeth thee.

Exod. 23:25-26

25 And ye shall serve the LORD your God, and he shall bless thy bread, and thy water; and I will take sickness away from the midst of thee

26 There shall nothing cast their young, nor be barren, in thy land: **the number of thy days I will fulfill.**

Ps. 84:11-12

11   **For the LORD God is a sun and shield; the LORD bestows favor and honor; no good thing does he withhold from those whose walk is blameless.**

12   O LORD Almighty, blessed is the man who trusts in you. (NIV)

The Lord bestows favor and honor, and no good thing does He withhold from those whose walk is blameless!

That scripture should motivate you to want to overcome sin, flesh and the devil.

Ps. 103:1-5

1   Bless the LORD, O my soul: and all that is within me, bless his holy name.

2   Bless the LORD, O my soul, and forget not all his benefits:

3   Who forgiveth all thine iniquities; who healeth all thy diseases;

4   Who redeemeth thy life from destruction; who crowneth thee with loving kindness and tender mercies;

5   Who satisfieth thy mouth with good things; so that thy youth is renewed like the eagles.

Ps. 107:19-20

19   Then they cry unto the LORD in their trouble, and he saveth them out of their distresses

20   He sent his word, and healed them, and delivered them from their destructions.

HOW DOES GOD FULFILL THESE PROMISES OF HEALTH AND DELIVERANCE?

Ps. 107:20
He sent his word, and healed them, and delivered them from their destruction's.

HE SENT HIS WORD! JESUS CHRIST, THE SON OF THE LIVING GOD, TO HEAL US! AND TO DELIVER US!
JESUS IS THE WORD, THE WORD IS SPIRIT, THE WORD IS THE SWORD OF THE SPIRIT, THE SWORD OF THE SPIRIT DEFEATS THE ENEMY, **THE SWORD OF THE SPIRIT IS THE WORD,**
THE WORD IS JESUS CHRIST, THE SON OF THE LIVING GOD! GLORY!

Jesus Christ was a living example of the will of God, He was and is the Word!
I recently had someone ask me if sickness was the will of God.
Sickness and disease, along with depression and oppression, is not from God. It never has been.
Wasn't Jesus the perfect will of God, manifest in the flesh?
If sickness or oppression came from God, and we are supposed to live with these infirmities, why would Jesus go about healing people and setting people free from oppression? That would have been against God's will.
Jesus only did the will of the Father, our Father.
If this were God's will, why wouldn't people pray to be sick? I think the answer is obvious. Satan wants to steal your healing and deliverance any way he can through the twins of doubt and unbelief, lies, stubbornness, or the traditions of men.
It is God's will for us to walk in divine health, divine healing, and divine power free from the strongholds of the enemy.
I have also heard people say that sickness glorifies God.

Matt. 9:2-8

2   And, behold, they brought to Him a man sick of the palsy, lying on a bed: and Jesus seeing their faith said unto the sick of the palsy; Son, be of good cheer; thy sins be forgiven thee

3   And, behold, certain of the scribes said within themselves, this man blasphemeth.

4   And Jesus knowing their thoughts said, wherefore think ye evil in your hearts?

5   For whether is easier, to say, Thy sins be forgiven thee, or to say, Arise, and walk?

6   But that ye may know that the Son of man hath power on earth to forgive sins, (then saith he to the sick of the palsy,) Arise, take up thy bed, and go unto thine house.

7   And he arose, and departed to his house.

8   But when the multitudes saw it, they marveled, and glorified God, which had given such power unto men.

THE MULTITUDES GLORIFIED GOD WHEN THE MAN WAS HEALED!

Sickness, pain, and our grief (oppression), is what Our Lord Jesus shed His precious blood for on the cross. The atoning work on the cross covers all our sickness and oppression, as well as our sin.

Why are believers sick? Why are believers oppressed? Why are believers living defeated lives? Why are believers bound by strongholds? Because today's believer does not recognize the enemy, and today's believer is living a life of passivity, calling it faith!

Today's believer is trying to believe their way to Spiritual freedom, instead of dealing with the enemy of their soul with the sword of the Spirit and Holy Ghost power... Because of this passivity, the enemy of our soul, Satan, is having a party accusing us day and night before our Father, as he is resurrecting the old man.

Satan has been defeated, he was defeated two thousand years ago at the cross, he is a *defeated foe!*

Most believers do not realize the DIVINE POWER that we have been given. Jesus knew we would have Spiritual battles in this life, which is why He has equipped us with the full armor of God. Jesus left us with all the power and authority to attain the victories, to attain the victorious and abundant life.

To have and maintain the victory over each onslaught of the enemy of our soul.

We have inherited divine weapons that are endued and saturated with divine power, a power that is much greater than any power of darkness!

Rom. 8:37-39

37   Nay, in all these things we are more than conquerors through him that loved us.

38   For I am persuaded, that neither death, nor life, nor angels, nor principalities, nor powers, nor things present, nor things to come,

39   Nor height, nor depth, nor any other creature, shall be able to separate us from the love of God, which is in Christ Jesus our Lord.

Matt. 11:12

And from the days of John the Baptist until now, the kingdom of heaven suffereth violence, and the violent take it by force (divine power). (An act of our will.)

THE LORD JESUS CHRIST HAS BESTOWED WEAPONS UPON US OF DIVINE POWER!

2 Cor. 10:4

For the weapons of our warfare are not carnal, but mighty through God to the pulling down of strong holds;

OUR MIGHTY WEAPONS OF WARFARE.

Divine power + divine weapons = the abundant life!

1   **the mighty power of the Blood of the Lamb**
2   **the mighty power of the Name of Jesus**
3   **the mighty power of the Word of God**
4   **the mighty power of the resurrection**

5	the mighty power of the Holy Ghost
6	the mighty power of praise and worship
7	the mighty power of binding and loosing
8	the mighty power of Holy Ghost prayer

WE SERVE AN ALMIGHTY GOD OF POWER!

When we stand in faith with these mighty weapons of warfare moving through our lips, we break through the strongholds and addictions of the enemy of our soul.

We tear down the strongholds of addiction, mental enemies, emotional enemies, physical enemies, and financial enemies.

The greater power of God almighty scatters the enemy with His mighty, divine power, working through His people.

As believers, we need to recognize our inheritance through Christ Jesus, while we are of use upon this earth.   Do not allow doubt and unbelief (the twins) to rob you of the wonderful freedom that has been paid for by the precious blood of the lamb.

The enemy is always lurking around the corner ready to overcome us if we do not recognize him for what he is.   Satan wants to deceive you, to lie to you so, that he can disarm you and then overcome you taking you captive.

The enemy has been defeated, he is a "has-been".

God wants us as believers to cooperate with Him by exercising our own free will, and by using the weapons that He has provided for us to be able to live the abundant life.

Deception opens the door for evil spirits to come into our lives.

Passivity provides a place for them to stay. The result of this combination will strengthen strongholds.

Knowledge of truth is therefore the first stage to freedom. God's truth will set you free.   As a believer, you must be willing to accept the truth concerning your particular situation in life. You must be true to your own heart. You must be willing to deal with the real you.

When you come to the revelation that you have a problem area in your life, you must decide to obey God's will, resist Satan's will, and exercise your own will to overcome the problem, and not be passive.

You must decide to act upon your God given free will to choose the future that you desire.

In Spiritual warfare, this will help you as you progress. You must use your will and choose the fight of freedom. You must use your will to resist strongholds and the wills of the flesh. When the enemy attacks you, you do not give him any ground. When the enemy tempts your flesh, you resist using the weapons God has provided for us.

By persevering, you will experience freedom in one area after another.

Persevere = A continued patient effort.   This is where you will make the decision that will affect your quality of life, and the quality of life of your loved ones.

You must choose to be ever passive, or choose to persevere, and not permit the enemy to manipulate you through strongholds and wills of the flesh any longer. This is a contest of the wills.   Through your God given free will, you must rise up and work actively with God to find total freedom.

As you do, you will begin to notice your resistance is having an effect on the enemy. The enemy has felt this pressure and will strike back.

As you persevere and exert pressure using God's mighty weapons, the enemy will leave.

As you patiently and progressively endure temptations and recapture the ground you have given to the enemy, you will find yourself progressively set free.

God wants us to be in total control of ourselves. To be able to use our God given free will to serve Him, without the hindrances of the enemy and the wills of the flesh.

1 Jn. 3:8
For this purpose the Son of God was manifested, that he might destroy the works of the devil.

Num. 23:19
God is not a man that He should lie; neither the son of man, that He should repent: hath He said, and shall He not do it? or hath he spoken, and shall he not make it good?

Phil. 2:9-10
9   Wherefore God also hath highly exalted Him, and given Him a name, which is above every name:
10   That at the name of Jesus every knee should bow, of things in heaven, and things in earth, and things under the earth;

When Jesus was resurrected, He was exalted far above all rule, authority, power, dominion, and every name that is named.

Eph.1:19-23
19   **And what is the exceeding greatness of his power to us**-ward who believe, according to the working of His mighty power,
20   **Which He wrought in Christ,** when He raised Him from the dead, and set Him at his own right hand in the heavenly places,
21   Far above all principality, power, might, dominion, and every name that is named, not only in this world, but also in that which is to come:
22   And hath put all things under His feet, and gave Him to be the Head over all things to the church,
23   Which is His body, the fullness of Him that filleth all in all.

We are His body, His hands, His feet, His mouth, and His voice in the earth.

Winning the battle is not the difficult part, it is recognizing the battle, the thoughts, the temptations, and the fiery darts, it is recognizing your weapons:

THE POWER OF REPENTANCE
THE POWER OF THE BLOOD OF THE LAMB
THE POWER IN THE NAME OF JESUS
THE POWER IN THE WORD OF GOD
THE POWER OF THE RESURRECTION
THE POWER OF THE HOLY GHOST
THE POWER OF PRAISE AND WORSHIP
THE POWER OF BINDING AND LOOSING
THE POWER OF HOLY GHOST PRAYER IN THE SPIRIT

IT IS RECOGNIZING THE ENEMY OF YOUR SOUL, SATAN AND HIS EVIL SPIRITS.

John 10:10
The thief cometh not, but for to steal, and to kill, and to destroy: I am come that they might have life, and that they might have it more abundantly".

"I AM COME THAT THEY MIGHT HAVE LIFE, AND THAT THEY MIGHT HAVE IT MORE ABUNDANTLY."
IF YOU ARE NOT HAVING LIFE, AND HAVING IT MORE ABUNDANTLY, THE THIEF HAS COME!   IT IS TIME FOR SPIRITUAL WAR!

Eph. 6:12-18

12 For we wrestle not against flesh and blood, but against principalities, against powers, against the rulers of the darkness of this world, against spiritual wickedness in high places.

13 Wherefore take unto you the whole armor of God that ye may be able to withstand in the evil day, and having done all, to stand.

14 Stand therefore, having your loins girt about with truth, and having on the breastplate of righteousness;

15 And your feet shod with the preparation of the gospel of peace;

16 Above all, taking the shield of faith, wherewith ye shall be able to quench all the fiery darts of the wicked

17 And take the helmet of salvation, and the sword of the Spirit, which is the word of God:

19 Praying always with all prayer and supplication in the Spirit, and watching thereunto with all perseverance and supplication for all saints;

Oh my God, in our Spiritual passivity, we have grieved, and are continuing to grieve, the Holy Ghost. If you cannot do something through us because of our disobedience to your will, then please Father, do something without us! Bypass us for a people who will act upon your Word!

THERE IS A DIVINE ORDER IN SPIRITUAL WARFARE

1) THE POWER OF REPENTANCE:

Rom. 3:23

For all have sinned, and come short of the glory of God;

2 Cor. 12:20-21

20 For I am afraid that when I come I may not find you as I want you to be, and you may not find me as you want me to be I fear that there may be quarreling, jealousy, outbursts of anger, factions, slander, gossip, arrogance and disorder.
  21 I am afraid that when I come again my God will humble me before you, and I will be grieved over many who have sinned earlier and have not repented of the impurity, sexual sin and debauchery in which they have indulged (NIV)

2) THE POWER OF PRAISE AND WORSHIP:

Ps. 149:6

Let the high praises of God be in their mouth, and a two-edged sword in their hand;

2 Chr. 20:21-22

21   And when he had consulted with the people, he appointed singers unto the LORD, and that should praise the beauty of holiness, as they went out before the army, and to say, Praise the LORD; for his mercy endureth forever.

22   And when they began to sing and to praise, the LORD set ambushments against the children of Ammon, Moab, and mount Seir, which were come against Judah; and they were smitten.

Ps. 18:3
I will call upon the LORD, who is worthy to be praised: so shall I be saved from mine enemies.

1 Cor. 14:15
What is it then? I will pray with the spirit, and I will pray with the understanding also: I will sing with the spirit, and I will sing with the understanding also.

3)   THE POWER OF THE HOLY GHOST AND PRAYER IN THE SPIRIT.

1 Cor. 14:15
What is it then? I will pray with the spirit, and I will pray with the understanding also: I will sing with the spirit, and I will sing with the understanding also.

Jude 1:20
But ye, beloved, building up yourselves on your most holy faith, praying in the Holy Ghost.

Rom. 8:26-27

26   Likewise, the Spirit also helpeth our infirmities (inabilities): for we know not what we should pray for as we ought: but the Spirit itself maketh intercession for us with groanings, which cannot be uttered.

27   And he that searcheth the hearts knoweth what is the mind of the Spirit, because he maketh intercession for the saints according to the will of God.

Eph. 6:18
Praying always with all prayer and supplication in the Spirit, and watching thereunto with all perseverance and supplication for all saints;

4)   THE POWER OF THE SPOKEN WORD OF GOD

THE WRITTEN RECORD THAT ENFORCES THE VICTORY BY THE BLOOD OF THE LAMB, AT THE CROSS, AT THE RESURRECTION, AT THE ASCENSION, AND OUR SEAT IN HEAVENLY PLACES, WITH CHRIST JESUS.

Heb. 4:12

For the word of God is quick, and powerful, and sharper than any two-edged sword, piercing even to the dividing asunder of soul and spirit, and of the joints and marrow, and is a discerner of the thoughts and intents of the heart.

Prov. 18:21
Death and life are in the power of the tongue:

Eccl. 8:4
Where the word of a king is, there is power:

Isa. 55:11
So shall my word be that goeth forth out of my mouth: it shall not return unto me void, but it shall accomplish that which I please, and it shall prosper in the thing whereto I sent it.

Jer. 1:12
Then said the LORD unto me, Thou hast well seen: for I will hasten my word to perform it.

Eph. 6:17
And take the helmet of salvation, and the sword of the Spirit, which is the word of God:

4)   THE POWER IN THE NAME OF JESUS:

John 14:14

If ye shall ask any thing in my name, I will do it.

Heb. 13:8

Jesus Christ the same yesterday, and today, and forever.

John 14:13

And whatsoever ye shall ask in my name, that will I do, that the Father may be glorified in the Son.

6)   THE POWER OF THE RESURRECTION:

Eph. 2:6

And hath raised us up together, and made us sit together in heavenly places in Christ Jesus.

Rom. 6:6
Knowing this, that our old man is crucified with him, that the body of sin might be destroyed, that henceforth we should not serve sin.

Rom. 6:11
Likewise reckon ye also yourselves to be dead indeed unto sin, but alive unto God through Jesus Christ our Lord.

2 Cor. 5:17
Therefore if any man be in Christ, he is a new creature: old things are passed away, behold, all things are become new.

7)   THE POWER OF BINDING AND LOOSING:

THE KEYS OF THE KINGDOM OF HEAVEN...WE BIND THE STRONGMAN, LOOSE THE WORD OF GOD, WEILD THE SWORD OF THE SPIRIT, AND SPEAK THE WRITTEN RECORD OF THE BLOOD OF THE LAMB.

Matt. 16:19
And I will give unto thee the keys of the kingdom of heaven: and whatsoever thou shalt bind on earth shall be bound in heaven: and whatsoever thou shalt loose on earth shall be loosed in heaven.

Matt. 18:18
Verily I say unto you, Whatsoever ye shall bind on earth shall be bound in heaven: and whatsoever ye shall loose on earth shall be loosed in heaven.

Mark 3:27
No man can enter into a strong man's house, and spoil his goods, except he will first bind the strong man; and then he will spoil his house.

Col. 2:15
And having spoiled principalities and powers, he made a shew of them openly, triumphing over them in it.

Eph. 6:12
For we wrestle not against flesh and blood, but against principalities, against powers, against the rulers of the darkness of this world, against spiritual wickedness in high places.

8)   THE POWER OF BLOOD OF THE LAMB:

THE WRITTEN RECORD ABOUT THE BLOOD OF THE LAMB.

Rev. 12:11
And they overcame him by the blood of the Lamb, and by the word of their testimony; and they loved not their lives unto the death.

Col. 1:13-15
13   Who hath delivered us from the power of darkness, and hath translated us into the kingdom of his dear Son:
14   In whom we have redemption through his blood, even the forgiveness of sins.

Heb. 9:14
How much more shall the blood of Christ, who through the eternal Spirit offered Himself without spot to God, purge your conscience from dead works to serve the living God?

Rom. 5:9
Much more then, being now justified by His blood, we shall be saved from wrath through Him.

Rev. 19:13
And He was clothed with a vesture dipped in blood: and His name is called The Word of God.

Isa. 40:21-31

21   Have ye not known? have ye not heard? Hath it not been told you from the beginning? have ye not understood from the foundations of the earth?

22   It is He that sitteth upon the circle of the earth, and the inhabitants thereof are as grasshoppers; that stretcheth out the heavens as a curtain, and spreadeth them out as a tent to dwell in:

23   That bringeth the princes to nothing; **(principalities, powers, rulers of darkness, spiritual wickedness)** he maketh the judges the adversary, **(Matt 5:25)** of the earth as vanity.

24   Yea, they shall not be planted; yea, they shall not be sown: yea, their stock shall not take root in the earth: and he shall also blow upon them, **(the Holy Ghost)** and they shall wither,**(the enemy, 2 Sam 22: 16-18)** and the whirlwind shall take them away as stubble

25   To whom then will ye liken me, or shall I be equal? saith the Holy One

26   Lift up your eyes on high, **(to God almighty)** and behold who hath created these things, **(the mighty ones, Joel 3: 11)** that bringeth out their host by number: he calleth them all by names by the greatness of his might, for that he is strong in power; not one faileth **(angels of the Lord).**

27   Why sayest thou, O Jacob, and speakest, O Israel, My way is hid from the LORD, and my judgment is passed over from my God?

28   Hast thou not known? hast thou not heard, that the everlasting God, the LORD, the Creator of the ends of the earth, fainteth not, neither is weary? there is no searching of his understanding.

29   He giveth power **(power of the Holy Ghost)** to the faint; and to them that have no might he increaseth strength **(by prayer in the Holy Ghost).**

30   Even the youths shall faint and be weary, and the young men shall utterly fall:

31   But they that wait **(to serve, as to wait upon tables)** upon the LORD shall renew their strength; they shall mount up with wings as eagles; they shall run, and not be weary; and they shall walk, and not faint

1 Cor. 2:9-14

9   But as it is written, Eye hath not seen, nor ear heard, neither have entered into the heart of man, the things which God hath prepared for them that love him.

10   But God hath revealed them unto us by his Spirit: for the Spirit searcheth all things, yea, the deep things of God

11   For what man knoweth the things of a man, save the spirit of man, which is in him? even so the things of God knoweth no man, but the Spirit of God.

12   Now we have received, not the spirit of the world, but the spirit which is of God; that we might know the things that are freely given to us of God.

13   Which things also we speak, not in the words which man's wisdom teacheth, but which the Holy Ghost teacheth; comparing spiritual things with spiritual.

14   But the natural man receiveth not the things of the Spirit of God: for they are foolishness unto him: neither can he know them, because they are spiritually discerned.

Reread and meditate on this document until you fully understand its entire content before moving on to document #10.

If you are having a problem understanding the content, pray and ask the Holy Spirit to enlighten the eyes of your understanding.

WATCHMAN RON

THE VOICE OF HIS BLOOD/document #10

Eph. 6:12-18

12   For we wrestle not against flesh and blood, but against principalities, against powers, against the rulers of the darkness of this world, against spiritual wickedness in high places.

13   Wherefore take unto you the whole armor of God that ye may be able to withstand in the evil day, and having done all, to stand.

14   Stand therefore, having your loins girt about with truth, and having on the breastplate of righteousness;

15   And your feet shod with the preparation of the gospel of peace;

16   Above all, taking the shield of faith, wherewith ye shall be able to quench all the fiery darts of the wicked.

17   And take the helmet of salvation, and the sword of the Spirit, which is the word of God:

18   Praying always with all prayer and supplication in the Spirit, and watching thereunto with all perseverance and supplication for all saints;

2 Cor. 10:5
Casting down imaginations and every high thing that exalteth itself against the knowledge of God, and bringing into captivity every thought to the obedience of Christ;

There is a divine order in spiritual warfare.

1)   REPENTANCE:

Rom. 3:23

For all have sinned, and come short of the glory of God;

2)   PRAISE AND WORSHIP:

Ps. 149:6

Let the high praises of God be in their mouth, and a two-edged sword in their hand;

3)   Holy Ghost prayer, in tongues and with the understanding:

4)   The Word of God:

The written record that enforces the victory by the Blood of the Lamb at the cross.

5)   The Name of Jesus:

John 14:14

If ye shall ask any thing in my name, I will do it.

6)   THE RESURRECTION:

Eph 2:6

And hath raised us up together, and made us sit together in heavenly places in Christ Jesus.

7)   BINDING AND LOOSING:

The keys of the kingdom of heaven.

We bind the strongman, loose the Word of God, wield the sword of the spirit, and speak the written record about the Blood of the Lamb.

8)   THE BLOOD OF THE LAMB

We speak the written word of God, which is the written record that enforces the victory over Satan and his hosts by the blood of the Lamb.

We decree God's will to be done, and through intercession, bind the stronghold and addiction and the forces of evil that hinder our walk of the new man in this life.

When we loose God's written word in the Name of Jesus, and pray in tongues we overcome the thoughts, temptations, and the wills of the flesh.

The battle of the wills, between our flesh and our spirit-man, is a daily battle. When God created us, he gave us a free will to choose daily whom we will serve. God gave HIS church, the believer, authority on this earth to be an overcomer of sin, flesh, and the devil.
Evil can be bound in the Name of Jesus. It is our use of the mighty powers of God, delegated to us in the Name of Jesus, that overcome evil with good. All things have been put under our feet.
We ascended with Christ Jesus to be seated with him in heavenly places. Born again, blood bought, spirit filled, children of God have been given a free will to reign in authority on earth, in this life, if we have the revelation of what we have been given! These come by an act of our God given free will, not by faith alone.

Instructions to overcome the enemy of your soul:

1   Repentance of sin from your heart.
2   High praises to the Lord, (thirty minutes to one hour).
3   In the Name of Jesus Christ of Nazareth and by the power of the Holy Ghost, bind Satan's principalities, powers, and rulers of darkness, his kings and nobles.
4   Bind your stronghold/addiction
       Example: bind spirit of lust, anger, spirit of infirmity, etc;
5   Loose the opposite.
       Example: loose freedom from lust, anger, spirit of infirmity, etc;

6   Wield the sword of the Spirit. (it is written)
7   Enforce that you have overcome him by the Blood of the Lamb.
8   Send Satan and his host back to the heavenlies.
9   Tell Satan the old man is dead and you are a new man in Christ Jesus.
10   In the Name of Jesus Christ of Nazareth and by the power of the

Holy Ghost, call upon the warring angels to come forth to form a protective hedge.

You are exercising your free will telling Satan and his host who you are in Christ Jesus. You have overcome him by the Blood of the Lamb…your old man is dead and you are a new man in Christ Jesus, and you are in the seat of authority in your life.

11   Bind & loose, speak the Word of God, pray in tongues, until you feel a release in your spirit. (approximately two hours daily in the beginning)

Prayer of repentance:

Father:
Have mercy on me to cleanse me of all my sins, in thought, word, deed, and wills of the flesh.

Wash me in the precious blood of the Lord Jesus Christ.

I believe that you raised Jesus from the dead, I confess that Jesus Christ is my Lord and Savior.

(Repentance; to have remorse for your sin, to change you mind and your ways, to turn away from your sinful past.)

Sample prayer
(After repentance and after high praises to the lord)
In the Name of JESUS CHRIST of Nazareth and by the power of the HOLY GHOST, Satan, I bind you.

In the Name of JESUS CHRIST of Nazareth, and by the Power of the HOLY GHOST, I bind your principalities, powers, and rulers of darkness.

In the Name of JESUS CHRIST of Nazareth, and by the Power of the HOLY GHOST, I bind your kings and nobles with chains and fetters of iron.

In the Name of JESUS CHRIST of Nazareth and by the Power of the HOLY   GHOST, I **bind** the strongman (stronghold)   of_____ and I **loose**_____.

For it is written, "I have overcome you devil **by the BLOOD OF THE LAMB**, and the word of my testimony!"

For it is written, "I have overcome you devil **by the BLOOD OF THE LAMB**, and the word of my testimony!"

You spirit of (stronghold), in the Name of JESUS CHRIST of Nazareth, and by the Power of the HOLY GHOST, I send you back to the heavenlies from whence you came, for you have no rights, no authority, no dominion here!

For it is written, "I have overcome you devil, **by the BLOOD OF THE LAMB**, and the word of my testimony!"

For it is written, "knowing this, that our old man is crucified with HIM."
For it is written, "for he that is dead is freed from sin, sickness and disease" The **old man is dead!** I am a new creature in CHRIST JESUS. **A new man in CHRIST JESUS!**

For it is written devil, "I have overcome you **by the BLOOD OF THE LAMB!"**

In the Name of JESUS CHRIST of Nazareth, and by the Power of the HOLY GHOST, I call upon the Mighty Ones, the Warring Angels, to come forth to form a protective hedge, to stand shoulder to shoulder with swords drawn to smite the enemy should they try to come around this ministry, my wife, my children, this marriage, this family, this home, our health, our finances, or the blessings and provisions of our LORD and KING the ALMIGHTY GOD!

For it is written, "I have overcome you devil, **by the BLOOD OF THE LAMB**, and the word of my testimony!"

It is written, "But GOD who is rich in mercy, for HIS great love wherewith, HE loved us, even when we were dead in sin, hath quickened us together with CHRIST, (by grace we are saved) and hath raised us up together, and made us sit together in heavenly places in CHRIST JESUS!"

PRAY IN THE HOLY GHOST [TONGUES]
Repeat prayer as needed, if the enemy bothers you with thoughts and fiery darts while you are praying, the enemy is still trying to resurrect your old man! The devil can be persistent, if you allow him to be so. Do not give him any ground, as he will try to hold his ground in the beginning!

REMEMBER, TO BE MILITANT, YOU ARE IN A WAR WITH THE ENEMY OF YOUR SOUL!

WATCHMAN RON

OVERCOMING POWERS OF DARKNESS
[personalize]
REPEAT DAILY

IT IS WRITTEN:
Rev. 12:11
And they overcame him by the blood of the Lamb, and by the word of their testimony; and they loved not their lives unto the death.
I have overcome you devil by the Blood of the lamb and the word of my testimony!

IT IS WRITTEN:
Eph. 1:7
In whom we have redemption through his blood, the forgiveness of sins, according to the riches of his grace;

IT IS WRITTEN:
Ps. 107:2
Let the redeemed of the LORD say so, whom he hath redeemed from the hand of the enemy;
Through the BLOOD OF JESUS, I am redeemed out of the hand of the enemy!

IT IS WRITTEN:
I Jn. 1:7
But if we walk in the light, as He is in the light, we have fellowship one with another, and the blood of Jesus Christ, His Son, cleanseth us from all sin.
Through the BLOOD OF JESUS all my sins are forgiven continually!

Rom. 5:9
Much more then, being now justified by his blood, we shall be saved from wrath through Him.

IT IS WRITTEN:
Rev. 12:11
And they overcame him by the blood of the Lamb, and by the word of their testimony; and they loved not their lives unto the death.

IT IS WRITTEN:
2 Cor. 5:21
For He hath made him to be sin for us, who knew no sin; that we might be made the righteousness of God in Him.

Heb. 13:12
Wherefore Jesus also, that he might sanctify the people with his own blood, suffered without the gate.
Through the BLOOD OF JESUS, I am justified, made righteous, and sanctified, daily!

1 Cor. 3:16
Know ye not that ye are the temple of God, and that the Spirit of God dwelleth in you?

Ps. 81:9

There shall no strange god be in thee; neither shalt thou worship any strange
   god.

2 Cor. 6:14

What communion hath light with darkness?

**THROUGH THE BLOOD OF JESUS, THE SON OF GOD, THE DEVIL HAS NO
PLACE IN ME, NO POWER OVER ME...BECAUSE OF ALL THAT JESUS
CHRIST DID FOR ME ON THE CROSS!**

IT IS WRITTEN: (Remember to personalize)
Rev. 12:11

**And they overcame him by the blood of the Lamb, and by the word of their
   testimony; and they loved not their lives unto the death.**

IT IS WRITTEN:
Rom. 6:3-12

4   Know ye not, that so many of us as were baptized into Jesus
       Christ were baptized into his death?
5   Therefore we are buried with him by baptism into death: that like
       as Christ was raised up from the dead by the glory of the Father,
       even so we also should walk in newness of life.
6   For if we have been planted together in the likeness of his death,
       we shall be also in the likeness of his resurrection:
7   Knowing this, that our old man is crucified with him, that the
       body of sin might be destroyed, that henceforth we should not
       serve sin
7   For he that is dead is freed from sin.
8   Now if we be dead with Christ, we believe that we shall also live
       with him:
9   Knowing that Christ being raised from the dead dieth no more;
       death hath no more dominion over him.
10   For in that He died, He died unto sin once: but in that He liveth,
       He liveth unto God.
11   Likewise reckon ye also yourselves to be dead indeed unto sin,
       but alive unto God through Jesus Christ our Lord
12   Let not sin therefore reign in your mortal body, that ye should
       obey it in the lusts thereof.

IT IS WRITTEN:
Eph. 2:4-6

4   But God, who is rich in mercy, for His great love wherewith He
     loved us,
5   Even when we were dead in sins, hath quickened us together with Christ, (by grace
     ye are saved;)
6   And hath raised us up together, and made us sit together in heavenly places in Christ
     Jesus:

IT IS WRITTEN: (Remember to personalize)
Rev. 12:11

11   And they overcame him by the blood of the Lamb, and by the word of their
testimony; and they loved not their lives unto the death.

THROUGH THE BLOOD OF JESUS, THE SON OF GOD, THE DEVIL HAS NO PLACE IN ME, NO POWER OVER ME...BECAUSE OF ALL THAT JESUS CHRIST DID FOR ME AT THE CROSS!

IT IS WRITTEN:
Rom. 6:5-7
5   For if we have been planted together in the likeness of His death,
    we shall be also in the likeness of His resurrection:
6   Knowing this, that our old man is crucified with Him, that the
    body of sin might be destroyed, that henceforth we should not serve
    sin.
7   For he that is dead is freed from sin.

Rom. 6:11
Likewise reckon ye also yourselves to be dead indeed unto sin, but alive   unto God through Jesus Christ our Lord.

EVIL SPIRITS HAVE NO AUTHORITY OVER A DEAD PERSON, AS MY OLD MAN (FLESH) IS CRUCIFIED WITH JESUS CHRIST ON THE CROSS! (Rom. 6:6)

IT IS WRITTEN:
Num.23:19
God is not a man that He should lie; neither the son of man that He should repent: hath He said, and shall He not do it? Or hath He spoken, and shall He not make it good?

IT IS WRITTEN:
Ps. 17:4
Concerning the works of men, by the word of thy lips (AN ACT OF OUR   WILL), I have kept me from the paths of the destroyer.

Ps. 119:89
Forever, O LORD, thy word is settled in heaven.

Prov. 18:21
Death and life are in the power of the tongue: (AN ACT OF OUR WILL.)

Eccl 8:4
Where the word of a king is, there is power:

Matt. 4:4
It is written, Man shall not live by bread alone, but by every word that proceedeth out of the mouth of God. (AN ACT OF OUR WILL)
Matt. 12:37
For by thy words thou shalt be justified, and by thy words thou shalt be condemned.

Matt. 24:35
Heaven and earth shall pass away, but my words shall not pass away.

John 15:7

If ye abide in me, and my words abide in you, ye shall ask what ye will, (AN ACT OF OUR WILL) and it shall be done unto you...

Heb. 4:12
For the word of God is quick, and powerful, and sharper than any two-edged sword, piercing even to the dividing asunder of soul and spirit, and of the joints and marrow, and is a discerner of the thoughts and intents of the heart.

1 Pet. 1:23
Being born again, not of corruptible seed, but of incorruptible, by the word of God, which liveth and abideth for ever.

You must enter into Spiritual warfare daily taking back your ground that the devil has stolen from you. Follow these God given instructions to the letter, as they were given to me from the Lord. Do not change the pattern, etc.; These Spiritual Instructions will set you free from STRONGHOLDS and the WILLS OF THE FLESH.
Reread and meditate on this document until you fully understand its entire content.
If you are having a problem understanding the content of any of the documents within this manual, pray and ask the Holy Spirit to enlighten the eyes of your understanding.

John 8:32
And ye shall know the truth, and the truth shall make you free.

God Bless You.
WATCHMAN RON

WORD from the LORD through Watchman Carol

For I shall bring forth my army with a mighty shout.

For my army is mighty and powerful.

I have prepared my army for such a time as this.

It is not by might nor by power, but by My Spirit, Thus saith the LORD your GOD.

Who was and is and is to come.

Call my name forth, call forth my army with me and as you do, the universe as you know it shall be changed.

All is part of my plan saith GOD.

Unto you this day is a day that I am glad in it, and as I come forth as the roaring lion of Judah, you my army will roar in the heavenlie's and will stop the enemy in his tracks.

My preparation for this time is in motion, so tarry not in your endeavor to roar with me, and the very angels in heaven will be watching over you my people.

STRONGHOLD OF ADDICTION

IT IS WRITTEN:

Rev 12:11
11 And they overcame him by the blood of the Lamb, and by the word of their testimony; and they loved not their lives unto the death

Prov 6:25
25   Lust not after her beauty in thine heart; neither let her take thee with her eyelids.

Matt 5:28
28   But I say unto you, That whosoever looketh on a woman to lust after her hath committed adultery with her already in his heart.

1 Cor 10:6
6   Now these things were our examples, to the intent we should not lust after evil things, as they also lusted.

Gal 5:16
16   This I say then, Walk in the Spirit, and ye shall not fulfill the lust of the flesh.

James 1:14-15
14   But every man is tempted, when he is drawn away of his own lust, and enticed.
15   Then when lust hath conceived, it bringeth forth sin: and sin, when it is finished, bringeth forth death.

2 Pet 1:4
4   Whereby are given unto us exceeding great and precious promises: that by these ye might be partakers of the divine nature, having escaped the corruption that is in the world through lust.

I Jn 2:16-17
16   For all that is in the world, the lust of the flesh, and the lust of the eyes, and the pride of life, is not of the Father, but is of the world.
    17 And the world passeth away, and the lust thereof: but he that doeth the will of God abideth forever.

STRONGHOLD OF ANGER

IT IS WRITTEN:

Rev 12:11
11 And they overcame him by the blood of the Lamb, and by the word of their testimony; and they loved not their lives unto the death

Ps 37:7-8
7 Rest in the LORD, and wait patiently for him: fret not thyself because of him who prospereth in his way, because of the man who bringeth wicked devices to pass
8 Cease from anger, and forsake wrath: fret not thyself in any wise to do evil.

Eccl 7:9
9 Be not hasty in thy spirit to be angry: for anger resteth in the bosom of fools

Eph 4:26-27
26 Be ye angry, and sin not: let not the sun go down upon your wrath:
27 Neither give place to the devil

Eph 4:29-31
29 Let no corrupt communication proceed out of your mouth, but that which is good to the use of edifying, that it may minister grace unto the hearers
30 And grieve not the holy Spirit of God, whereby ye are sealed unto the day of redemption
31 Let all bitterness, and wrath, and anger, and clamour, and evil speaking, be put away from you, with all malice:

Col 3:8
8 But now ye also put off all these; anger, wrath, malice, blasphemy, filthy communication out of your mouth

Prov 16:32
32 He that is slow to anger is better than the mighty; and he that ruleth his spirit than he that taketh a city

Prov 25:28
28 He that hath no rule over his own spirit is like a city that is broken down, and without walls

STRONGHOLD OF ANXIETY

IT IS WRITTEN:

Rev 12:11
11 And they overcame him by the blood of the Lamb, and by the word of their testimony; and they loved not their lives unto the death

Matt 6:33
33 But seek ye first the kingdom of God, and his righteousness; and all these things shall be added unto you

Matt 6:34
34 Take therefore no thought for the morrow: for the morrow shall take thought for the things of itself Sufficient unto the day is the evil thereof

Phil 4:6-9
6 Be careful for nothing; but in everything by prayer and supplication with thanksgiving let your requests be made known unto God
7 And the peace of God, which passeth all understanding, shall keep your hearts and minds through Christ Jesus
8 Finally, brethren, whatsoever things are true, whatsoever things are honest, whatsoever things are just, whatsoever things are pure, whatsoever things are lovely, whatsoever things are of good report; if there be any virtue, and if there be any praise, think on these things
9 Those things, which ye have both learned, and received, and heard, and seen in me, do: and the God of peace shall be with you

1 Pet 5:7
7 Casting all your care upon him; for he careth for you

Dan 4:2-3
2 I thought it good to shew the signs and wonders that the high God hath wrought toward me
3 How great are his signs! and how mighty are his wonders! his kingdom is an everlasting kingdom, and his dominion is from generation to generation

Matt 6:27
Which of you by taking thought can add one cubit unto his stature?

STRONGHOLD OF BITTERNESS

IT IS WRITTEN:

Rev 12:11
11 And they overcame him by the blood of the Lamb, and by the word of their testimony; and they loved not their lives unto the death

Eph 4:29-31
29 Let no corrupt communication proceed out of your mouth, but that which is good to the use of edifying, that it may minister grace unto the hearers
30 And grieve not the holy Spirit of God, whereby ye are sealed unto the day of redemption
31 Let all bitterness, and wrath, and anger, and clamor, and evil speaking, be put away from you, with all malice:

Heb 12:15
15 Looking diligently lest any man fail of the grace of God; lest any root of bitterness springing up trouble you, and thereby many be defiled;

Col 3:13-16
13 Forbearing one another, and forgiving one another, if any man have a quarrel against any: even as Christ forgave you, so also do ye
14 And above all these things put on charity, which is the bond of perfectness
15 And let the peace of God rule in your hearts, to the which also ye are called in one body; and be ye thankful
16 Let the word of Christ dwell in you richly in all wisdom; teaching and admonishing one another in psalms and hymns and spiritual songs, singing with grace in your hearts to the Lord

Matt 5:44
44 But I say unto you, Love your enemies, bless them that curse you, do good to them that hate you, and pray for them which despitefully use you, and persecute you;

Matt 6:14-15
14 For if ye forgive men their trespasses, your heavenly Father will also forgive you:
15 But if ye forgive not men their trespasses, neither will your Father forgive your trespasses

STRONGHOLD OF THE CHALDEANS,PSYCHICS,WITCHCRAFT,

IT IS WRITTEN:

Rev 12:11
11 And they overcame him by the blood of the Lamb, and by the word of their testimony; and they loved not their lives unto the death

Lev 19:31
31 Regard not them that have familiar spirits, neither seek after wizards, to be defiled by them: I am the LORD your God

Deut 7:25-26
25 The graven images of their gods shall ye burn with fire: thou shalt not desire the silver or gold that is on them, nor take it unto thee, lest thou be snared therein: for it is an abomination to the LORD thy God
26 Neither shalt thou bring an abomination into thine house, lest thou be a cursed thing like it: but thou shalt utterly detest it, and thou shalt utterly abhor it; for it is a cursed thing

Deut 18:10-12
10 There shall not be found among you any one that maketh his son or his daughter to pass through the fire, or that useth divination, or an observer of times, or an enchanter, or a witch,
11 Or a charmer, or a consulter with familiar spirits, or a wizard, or a necromancer
12 For all that do these things are an abomination unto the LORD: and because of these abominations the LORD thy God doth drive them out from before thee

Isa 47:13-14
13 Thou art wearied in the multitude of thy counsels Let now the astrologers, the stargazers, the monthly prognosticators, stand up, and save thee from these things that shall come upon thee
14 Behold, they shall be as stubble; the fire shall burn them; they shall not deliver themselves from the power of the flame: there shall not be a coal to warm at, nor fire to sit before it

Acts 19:19
19 Many of them also which used curious arts brought their books together, and burned them before all men: and they counted the price of them, and found it fifty thousand pieces of silver

STRONGHOLD OF CONDEMNATION

IT IS WRITTEN:

Rev 12:11
11 And they overcame him by the blood of the Lamb, and by the word of their testimony; and they loved not their lives unto the death

John 3:17-18
17 For God sent not his Son into the world to condemn the world; but that the world through him might be saved
18 He that believeth on him is not condemned: but he that believeth not is condemned already, because he hath not believed in the name of the only begotten Son of God

John 5:24
24 Verily, verily, I say unto you, He that heareth my word, and believeth on him that sent me, hath everlasting life, and shall not come into condemnation; but is passed from death unto life

Rom 8:1-2
1 There is therefore now no condemnation to them which are in Christ Jesus, who walk not after the flesh, but after the Spirit
2 For the law of the Spirit of life in Christ Jesus hath made me free from the law of sin and death

Ps 37:32-33
32 The wicked watcheth the righteous, and seeketh to slay him
33 The LORD will not leave him in his hand, nor condemn him when he is judged

Ps 94:21-23
21 They gather themselves together against the soul of the righteous, and condemn the innocent blood
22 But the LORD is my defense; and my God is the rock of my refuge
23 And he shall bring upon them their own iniquity, and shall cut them off in their own wickedness; yea, the LORD our God shall cut them off

Ps 109:31
31 For he shall stand at the right hand of the poor, to save him from those that condemn his soul

STRONGHOLD OF CONFUSION

IT IS WRITTEN:

Rev 12:11
11 And they overcame him by the blood of the Lamb, and by the word of their testimony; and they loved not their lives unto the death

Ps 35:4
4 Let them be confounded and put to shame that seek after my soul: let them be turned back and brought to confusion that devise my hurt

Ps 35:26
26 Let them be ashamed and brought to confusion together that rejoice at mine hurt: let them be clothed with shame and dishonor that magnify themselves against me

Ps 70:2
2 Let them be ashamed and confounded that seek after my soul: let them be turned backward, and put to confusion, that desire my hurt

Ps 71:1
1 In thee, O LORD, do I put my trust: let me never be put to confusion

Ps 109:29
29 Let mine adversaries be clothed with shame, and let them cover themselves with their own confusion, as with a mantle

1 Cor 14:33
33 For God is not the author of confusion, but of peace, as in all churches of the saints

James 3:16
16 For where envying and strife is, there is confusion and every evil work

1 Pet 2:6
6 Wherefore also it is contained in the scripture, Behold, I lay in Sion a chief corner stone, elect, precious: and he that believeth on him shall not be confounded
Jer 17;18 Let them be confounded that persecute me, but let not me be confounded:

STRONGHOLD OF COVETOUSNESS

IT IS WRITTEN:

Rev 12:11
11 And they overcame him by the blood of the Lamb, and by the word of their testimony;
and they loved not their lives unto the death

Exod 20:17
17 Thou shalt not covet thy neighbor's house, thou shalt not covet thy neighbor's wife,
nor his manservant, nor his maidservant, nor his ox, nor his ass, nor any thing that is thy
neighbor's

Matt 5:28
28 But I say unto you, That whosoever looketh on a woman to lust after her hath
committed adultery with her already in his heart

Luke 12:15
15 And he said unto them, Take heed, and beware of covetousness: for a man's life
consisteth not in the abundance of the things which he possesseth

Acts 20:33
33 I have coveted no man's silver, or gold, or apparel

I Jn 2:15-17
15 Love not the world, neither the things that are in the world If any man love the world,
the love of the Father is not in him
16 For all that is in the world, the lust of the flesh, and the lust of the eyes, and the pride
of life, is not of the Father, but is of the world
17 And the world passeth away, and the lust thereof: but he that doeth the will of God
abideth for ever

Col 3:5-6
5 Mortify therefore your members which are upon the earth; fornication, uncleanness,
inordinate affection, evil concupiscence, and covetousness, which is idolatry:
6 For which things' sake the wrath of God cometh on the children of disobedience:

1 Cor 12:31
31 But covet earnestly the best gifts: and yet shew I unto you a more excellent way

STRONGHOLD OF CRITICISM

IT IS WRITTEN:

Rev 12:11
11 And they overcame him by the blood of the Lamb, and by the word of their testimony; and they loved not their lives unto the death

2 Chr 19:6
6 Take heed what ye do: for ye judge not for man, but for the LORD, who is with you in the judgment

Matt 7:1-5
1 Judge not, that ye be not judged
2 For with what judgment ye judge, ye shall be judged: and with what measure ye mete, it shall be measured to you again
3 And why beholdest thou the mote that is in thy brother's eye, but considerest not the beam that is in thine own eye?
4 Or how wilt thou say to thy brother, Let me pull out the mote out of thine eye; and, behold, a beam is in thine own eye?
5 Thou hypocrite, first cast out the beam out of thine own eye; and then shalt thou see clearly to cast out the mote out of thy brother's eye

Luke 6:37
37 Judge not, and ye shall not be judged: condemn not, and ye shall not be condemned: forgive, and ye shall be forgiven:

Rom 2:1
1 Therefore thou art inexcusable, O man, whosoever thou art that judgest: for wherein thou judgest another, thou condemnest thyself; for thou that judgest doest the same things

Rom 14:13
13 Let us not therefore judge one another any more: but judge this rather, that no man put a stumbling block or an occasion to fall in his brother's way

1 Cor 4:5
5 Therefore judge nothing before the time, until the Lord come, who both will bring to light the hidden things of darkness, and will make manifest the counsels of the hearts: and then shall every man have praise of God

STRONGHOLD OF DEPRESSION

IT IS WRITTEN:

Rev 12:11
11 And they overcame him by the blood of the Lamb, and by the word of their testimony; and they loved not their lives unto the death

Deut 26:7-8
7 And when we cried unto the LORD God of our fathers, the LORD heard our voice, and looked on our affliction, and our labor, and our oppression:
8 And the LORD brought us forth out of Egypt with a mighty hand, and with an outstretched arm, and with great terribleness, and with signs, and with wonders:

Job 36:15
15 He delivereth the poor in his affliction, and openeth their ears in oppression

Isa 54:14
14 In righteousness shalt thou be established: thou shalt be far from oppression; for thou shalt not fear: and from terror; for it shall not come near thee

Ezek 46:18
18 Moreover the prince shall not take of the people's inheritance by oppression to thrust them out of their possession;

Job 22:29
29 When men are cast down, then thou shalt say, There is lifting up; and he shall save the humble person

Ps 37:24
24 Though he fall, he shall not be utterly cast down: for the LORD upholdeth him with his hand

2 Cor 4:9
9 Persecuted, but not forsaken; cast down, but not destroyed;

2 Cor 7:6
6 Nevertheless God, that comforteth those that are cast down,

STRONGHOLD OF DISCOURAGEMENT

IT IS WRITTEN:

Rev 12:11
11 And they overcame him by the blood of the Lamb, and by the word of their testimony; and they loved not their lives unto the death

Num 13:20
20 And what the land is, whether it be fat or lean, whether there be wood therein, or not And be ye of good courage,

Deut 31:6
6 Be strong and of a good courage, fear not, nor be afraid of them: for the LORD thy God, he it is that doth go with thee; he will not fail thee, nor forsake thee

Josh 1:9
9 Have not I commanded thee? Be strong and of a good courage; be not afraid, neither be thou dismayed: for the LORD thy God is with thee whithersoever thou goest

Josh 10:25
25 And Joshua said unto them, Fear not, nor be dismayed, be strong and of good courage: for thus shall the LORD do to all your enemies against whom ye fight

1 Chr 28:20
20 And David said to Solomon his son, Be strong and of good courage, and do it: fear not, nor be dismayed: for the LORD God, even my God, will be with thee; he will not fail thee, nor forsake thee,

Ps 27:14
14 Wait on the LORD: be of good courage, and he shall strengthen thine heart: wait, I say, on the LORD

Ps 31:24
24 Be of good courage, and he shall strengthen your heart, all ye that hope in the LORD

STRONGHOLD OF DISEASE

IT IS WRITTEN:

Rev 12:11
11 And they overcame him by the blood of the Lamb, and by the word of their testimony; and they loved not their lives unto the death

Isa 53:5
5 But he was wounded for our transgressions, he was bruised for our iniquities: the chastisement of our peace was upon him; and with his stripes we are healed

1 Pet 2:24
24 Who his own self bare our sins in his own body on the tree, that we, being dead to sins, should live unto righteousness: by whose stripes ye were healed

Matt 8:7
7 And Jesus saith unto him, I will come and heal him

Matt 10:1
1 And when he had called unto him his twelve disciples, he gave them power against unclean spirits, to cast them out, and to heal all manner of sickness and all manner of disease

Luke 4:18
18 The Spirit of the Lord is upon me, because he hath anointed me to preach the gospel to the poor; he hath sent me to heal the brokenhearted, to preach deliverance to the captives, and recovering of sight to the blind, to set at liberty them that are bruised,

Luke 9:2
2 And he sent them to preach the kingdom of God, and to heal the sick

Luke 10:9
9 And heal the sick that are therein, and say unto them, The kingdom of God is come nigh unto you

Acts 4:30
30 By stretching forth thine hand to heal; and that signs and wonders may be done by the name of thy holy child Jesus

STRONGHOLD OF DISOBEDIENCE

IT IS WRITTEN:

Rev 12:11
11 And they overcame him by the blood of the Lamb, and by the word of their testimony; and they loved not their lives unto the death

1 Sam 15:23
23 For rebellion is as the sin of witchcraft, and stubbornness is as iniquity and idolatry Because thou hast rejected the word of the LORD, he hath also rejected thee from being king

Job 34:37
37 For he addeth rebellion unto his sin, he clappeth his hands among us, and multiplieth his words against God

Prov 17:11
11 An evil man seeketh only rebellion: therefore a cruel messenger shall be sent against him

Rom 6:16
16 Know ye not, that to whom ye yield yourselves servants to obey, his servants ye are to whom ye obey; whether of sin unto death, or of obedience unto righteousness?

2 Cor 10:5
5 Casting down imaginations, and every high thing that exalteth itself against the knowledge of God, and bringing into captivity every thought to the obedience of Christ;

2 Cor 10:6
6 And having in a readiness to revenge all disobedience, when your obedience is fulfilled

Heb 5:8
8 Though he were a Son, yet learned he obedience by the things which he suffered;

STRONGHOLD OF DISTRESS

IT IS WRITTEN:

Rev 12:11
11 And they overcame him by the blood of the Lamb, and by the word of their testimony; and they loved not their lives unto the death

Ps 17:13-15
13 Arise, O LORD, disappoint him, cast him down: deliver my soul from the wicked, which is thy sword:
14 From men which are thy hand, O LORD, from men of the world, which have their portion in this life, and whose belly thou fillest with thy hid treasure: they are full of children, and leave the rest of their substance to their babes
15 As for me, I will behold thy face in righteousness: I shall be satisfied, when I awake, with thy likeness

Ps 22:4
4 Our fathers trusted in thee: they trusted, and thou didst deliver them

Ps 31:1
1 In thee, O LORD, do I put my trust; let me never be ashamed: deliver me in thy righteousness

Ps 31:2
2 Bow down thine ear to me; deliver me speedily: be thou my strong rock, for an house of defence to save me

Ps 33:18-21
18 Behold, the eye of the LORD is upon them that fear him, upon them that hope in his mercy;
19 To deliver their soul from death, and to keep them alive in famine
20 Our soul waiteth for the LORD: he is our help and our shield
21 For our heart shall rejoice in him, because we have trusted in his holy name

Ps 37:40
40 And the LORD shall help them, and deliver them: he shall deliver them from the wicked, and save them, because they trust in him

The LORD will preserve him, and keep him alive; and he shall be blessed

STRONGHOLD OF DOUBT

IT IS WRITTEN:

Rev 12:11
11 And they overcame him by the blood of the Lamb, and by the word of their testimony; and they loved not their lives unto the death

Matt 21:21
21 Jesus answered and said unto them, Verily I say unto you, If ye have faith, and doubt not, ye shall not only do this which is done to the fig tree, but also if ye shall say unto this mountain, Be thou removed, and be thou cast into the sea; it shall be done

Matt 21:22
22 And all things, whatsoever ye shall ask in prayer, believing, ye shall receive

Rom 12:3
3 God hath dealt to every man the measure of faith

Heb 4:14-15
14 Seeing then that we have a great high priest, that is passed into the heavens, Jesus the Son of God, let us hold fast our profession
15 For we have not an high priest which cannot be touched with the feeling of our infirmities; but was in all points tempted like as we are, yet without sin

Matt 9:22
22 But Jesus turned him about, and when he saw her, he said, Daughter, be of good comfort; thy faith hath made thee whole

Matt 17:20
20 If ye have faith as a grain of mustard seed, ye shall say unto this mountain, Remove hence to yonder place; and it shall remove; and nothing shall be impossible unto you

Rom 5:1
1 Therefore being justified by faith, we have peace with God through our Lord Jesus Christ:

STRONGHOLD OF FEAR

IT IS WRITTEN:
Rev 12:11
11 And they overcame him by the blood of the Lamb, and by the word of their testimony; and they loved not their lives unto the death

Deut 1:21
21 Behold, the LORD thy God hath set the land before thee: go up and possess it, as the LORD God of thy fathers hath said unto thee; fear not, neither be discouraged

Deut 31:6
6 fear not, nor be afraid of them: for the LORD thy God, he it is that doth go with thee; he will not fail thee, nor forsake thee

Josh 8:1
1 And the LORD said unto Joshua, Fear not, neither be thou dismayed: take all the people of war with thee,

Josh 10:25
25 And Joshua said unto them, Fear not, nor be dismayed, be strong and of good courage: for thus shall the LORD do to all your enemies against whom ye fight

1 Sam 12:20
20 And Samuel said unto the people, Fear not: ye have done all this wickedness: yet turn not aside from following the LORD, but serve the LORD with all your heart;

Josh 8:1
1 and the LORD said unto Joshua, Fear not, neither be thou dismayed: take all the people of war with thee,

Josh 10:25
25 And Joshua said unto them, Fear not, nor be dismayed, be strong and of good courage: for thus shall the LORD do to all your enemies against whom ye fight

STRONGHOLD OF GREED

IT IS WRITTEN:

Rev 12:11
11 And they overcame him by the blood of the Lamb, and by the word of their testimony; and they loved not their lives unto the death

Gen 30:28
28 And he said, Appoint me thy wages, and I will give it

Gen 42:25
25 Then Joseph commanded to fill their sacks with corn, and to restore every man's money into his sack, and to give them provision for the way: and thus did he unto them

Gen 48:4
4 And said unto me, Behold, I will make thee fruitful, and multiply thee, and I will make of thee a multitude of people; and will give this land to thy seed after thee for an everlasting possession

II Ki 5:22
22 And he said, All is well My master hath sent me, saying, Behold, even now there be come to me from mount Ephraim two young men of the sons of the prophets: give them, I pray thee, a talent of silver, and two changes of garments

Ps 29:1-2
1 Give unto the LORD, O ye mighty, give unto the LORD glory and strength
2 Give unto the LORD the glory due unto his name; worship the LORD in the beauty of holiness

Jer 17:10
10 I the LORD search the heart, I try the reins, even to give every man according to his ways, and according to the fruit of his doings

Matt 5:42
42 Give to him that asketh thee, and from him that would borrow of thee turn not thou away

STRONGHOLD OF GUILT

IT IS WRITTEN:

Rev 12:11
11 And they overcame him by the blood of the Lamb, and by the word of their testimony; and they loved not their lives unto the death

Acts 13:37-39
37 But he, whom God raised again, saw no corruption
38 Be it known unto you therefore, men and brethren, that through this man is preached unto you the forgiveness of sins:
39 And by him all that believe are justified from all things, from which ye could not be justified by the law of Moses

Rom 3:23-24
23 For all have sinned, and come short of the glory of God;
24 Being justified freely by his grace through the redemption that is in Christ Jesus:

Rom 5:1
1 Therefore being justified by faith, we have peace with God through our Lord Jesus Christ:

Rom 5:8-9
8 But God commendeth his love toward us, in that, while we were yet sinners, Christ died for us
9 Much more then, being now justified by his blood, we shall be saved from wrath through him

1 Cor 1:30
30 But of him are ye in Christ Jesus, who of God is made unto us wisdom, and righteousness, and sanctification, and redemption:

John 3:17
17 For God sent not his Son into the world to condemn the world; but that the world through him might be saved

Rom 3:25
25 Whom God hath set forth to be a propitiation through faith in his blood, to declare his righteousness for the remission of sins that are past, through the forbearance of God;

STRONGHOLD OF HEARTACHE

IT IS WRITTEN:
Rev 12:11
11 And they overcame him by the blood of the Lamb, and by the word of their testimony; and they loved not their lives unto the death

Josh 14:8
8 Nevertheless my brethren that went up with me made the heart of the people melt: but I wholly followed the LORD my God

Josh 24:23
23 Now therefore put away, said he, the strange gods which are among you, and incline your heart unto the LORD God of Israel

Judg 19:6
6 Be content, I pray thee, and tarry all night, and let thine heart be merry

1 Sam 2:1
1 And Hannah prayed, and said, My heart rejoiceth in the LORD, mine horn is exalted in the LORD: my mouth is enlarged over mine enemies; because I rejoice in thy salvation

1 Sam 12:24
24 Only fear the LORD, and serve him in truth with all your heart: for consider how great things he hath done for you

Ps 7:10
10 My defence is of God, which saveth the upright in heart

Ps 9:1
1 I will praise thee, O LORD, with my whole heart; I will shew forth all thy marvelous works

Ps 10:6
6 He hath said in his heart, I shall not be moved: for I shall never be in adversity

Ps 10:17
17 LORD, thou hast heard the desire of the humble: thou wilt prepare their heart, thou wilt cause thine ear to hear:

STRONGHOLD OF IMPATIENCE

IT IS WRITTEN:

Rev 12:11
11 And they overcame him by the blood of the Lamb, and by the word of their testimony; and they loved not their lives unto the death

Eccl 7:8
8 Better is the end of a thing than the beginning thereof: and the patient in spirit is better than the proud in spirit

Prov 16:32
32 He that is slow to anger is better than the mighty; and he that ruleth his spirit than he that taketh a city

Luke 21:19
19 In your patience possess ye your souls

Luke 8:15
15 But that on the good ground are they, which in an honest and good heart, having heard the word, keep it, and bring forth fruit with patience

Rom 15:4
4 For whatsoever things were written aforetime were written for our learning, that we through patience and comfort of the scriptures might have hope

Col 1:11
11 Strengthened with all might, according to his glorious power, unto all patience and longsuffering with joyfulness;

1Thes 1:3
3 Remembering without ceasing your work of faith, and labour of love, and patience of hope in our Lord Jesus Christ, in the sight of God and our Father;

Heb 12:1
1 Wherefore seeing we also are compassed about with so great a cloud of witnesses, let us lay aside every weight, and the sin which doth so easily beset us, and let us run with patience the race that is set before us,

STRONGHOLD OF INFERIORITY

IT IS WRITTEN:

Rev 12:11
11 And they overcame him by the blood of the Lamb, and by the word of their testimony; and they loved not their lives unto the death

Ps 118:8-11
8 It is better to trust in the LORD than to put confidence in man
9 It is better to trust in the LORD than to put confidence in princes
10 All nations compassed me about: but in the name of the LORD will I destroy them
11 They compassed me about; yea, they compassed me about: but in the name of the LORD I will destroy them

Prov 3:26
26 For the LORD shall be thy confidence, and shall keep thy foot from being taken

Isa 30:15
15 For thus saith the Lord GOD, the Holy One of Israel; In returning and rest shall ye be saved; in quietness and in confidence shall be your strength:

Ps 118:8-11
8 It is better to trust in the LORD than to put confidence in man
9 It is better to trust in the LORD than to put confidence in princes
10 All nations compassed me about: but in the name of the LORD will I destroy them
11 They compassed me about; yea, they compassed me about: but in the name of the LORD I will destroy them

Prov 3:26
26 For the LORD shall be thy confidence, and shall keep thy foot from being taken

Eph 3:12
12 In whom we have boldness and access with confidence by the faith of him

STRONGHOLD OF INSECURITY

IT IS WRITTEN:

Rev 12:11
11 And they overcame him by the blood of the Lamb, and by the word of their testimony; and they loved not their lives unto the death

Job 11:19
19 Also thou shalt lie down, and none shall make thee afraid; yea, many shall make suit unto thee

Ps 3:3-6
3 But thou, O LORD, art a shield for me; my glory, and the lifter up of mine head
4 I cried unto the LORD with my voice, and he heard me out of his holy hill Selah
5 I laid me down and slept; I awaked; for the LORD sustained me
6 I will not be afraid of ten thousands of people, that have set themselves against me round about

Ps 4:8
8 I will both lay me down in peace, and sleep: for thou, LORD, only makest me dwell in safety

Prov 3:24-26
24 When thou liest down, thou shalt not be afraid: yea, thou shalt lie down, and thy sleep shall be sweet
25 Be not afraid of sudden fear, neither of the desolation of the wicked, when it cometh
26 For the LORD shall be thy confidence, and shall keep thy foot from being taken

Ps 27:3
3 Though an host should encamp against me, my heart shall not fear: though war should rise against me, in this will I be confident

Phil 1:6
6 Being confident of this very thing, that he which hath begun a good work in you will perform it until the day of Jesus Christ:

STRONGHOLD OF JUDGMENT

IT IS WRITTEN:

Rev 12:11
11 And they overcame him by the blood of the Lamb, and by the word of their testimony; and they loved not their lives unto the death

Matt 7:1-2
1 Judge not, that ye be not judged
2 For with what judgment ye judge, ye shall be judged: and with what measure ye mete, it shall be measured to you again

Matt 7:3
3 And why beholdest thou the mote that is in thy brother's eye, but considerest not the beam that is in thine own eye?

Luke 6:37
37 Judge not, and ye shall not be judged: condemn not, and ye shall not be condemned: forgive, and ye shall be forgiven:

Luke 6:38
38 Give, and it shall be given unto you; good measure, pressed down, and shaken together, and running over, shall men give into your bosom For with the same measure that ye mete withal it shall be measured to you again

John 7:24
24 Judge not according to the appearance, but judge righteous judgment

Rom 14:13
13 Let us not therefore judge one another anymore: but judge this rather, that no man put a stumblingblock or an occasion to fall in his brother's way

Rom 14:10
10 But why dost thou judge thy brother? or why dost thou set at nought thy brother? for we shall all stand before the judgment seat of Christ

Gal 6:1
1 Brethren, if a man be overtaken in a fault, ye which are spiritual, restore such an one in the spirit of meekness; considering thyself, lest thou also be tempted

STRONGHOLD OF LYING

IT IS WRITTEN:

Rev 12:11
11 And they overcame him by the blood of the Lamb, and by the word of their testimony; and they loved not their lives unto the death

Josh 24:14
14 Now therefore fear the LORD, and serve him in sincerity and in truth:

1 Sam 12:24
24 Only fear the LORD, and serve him in truth with all your heart: for consider how great things he hath done for you

IKing 2:4
4 That the LORD may continue his word which he spake concerning me, saying, If thy children take heed to their way, to walk before me in truth with all their heart and with all their soul, there shall not fail thee

Ps 15:1-2
1 LORD, who shall abide in thy tabernacle? who shall dwell in thy holy hill?
2 He that walketh uprightly, and worketh righteousness, and speaketh the truth in his heart

Ps 25:5
5 Lead me in thy truth, and teach me: for thou art the God of my salvation; on thee do I wait all the day

Ps 43:3-4
3 O send out thy light and thy truth: let them lead me; let them bring me unto thy holy hill, and to thy tabernacles
4 Then will I go unto the altar of God, unto God my exceeding joy: yea, upon the harp will I praise thee, O God my God

Ps 45:4
4 And in thy majesty ride prosperously because of truth and meekness and righteousness; and thy right hand shall teach thee terrible things

STRONGHOLD OF LOW SELF ESTEEM

IT IS WRITTEN:

Rev 12:11
11 And they overcame him by the blood of the Lamb, and by the word of their testimony; and they loved not their lives unto the death

Job 4:7-9
7 Remember, I pray thee, whoever perished, being innocent? or where were the righteous cut off?
8 Even as I have seen, they that plow iniquity, and sow wickedness, reap the same
9 By the blast of God they perish, and by the breath of his nostrils are they consumed

Prov 3:26
26 For the LORD shall be thy confidence, and shall keep thy foot from being taken

Prov 14:26
26 In the fear of the LORD is strong confidence: and his children shall have a place of refuge

Isa 30:15
15 For thus saith the Lord GOD, the Holy One of Israel; In returning and rest shall ye be saved; in quietness and in confidence shall be your strength: and ye would not

Micah 7:7
7 Therefore I will look unto the LORD; I will wait for the God of my salvation: my God will hear me

Eph 3:12
12 In whom we have boldness and access with confidence by the faith of him

Phil 1:25
25 And having this confidence, I know that I shall abide and continue with you all for your furtherance and joy of faith;

fast the confidence and the rejoicing of the hope firm unto the end

STRONGHOLD OF MATERIALISM

IT IS WRITTEN:

Rev 12:11
11 And they overcame him by the blood of the Lamb, and by the word of their testimony; and they loved not their lives unto the death

Ps 96:5
5 For all the gods of the nations are idols: but the LORD made the heavens

Ps 106:36
36 And they served their idols: which were a snare unto them

Ps 115:3-4
3 But our God is in the heavens: he hath done whatsoever he hath pleased
4 Their idols are silver and gold, the work of men's hands

Isa 2:8
8 Their land also is full of idols; they worship the work of their own hands, that which their own fingers have made:

I Jn 5:21
21 Little children, keep yourselves from idols Amen

Rev 3:14-22
14 And unto the angel of the church of the Laodiceans write; These things saith the Amen, the faithful and true witness, the beginning of the creation of God;
15 I know thy works, that thou art neither cold nor hot: I would thou wert cold or hot
16 So then because thou art lukewarm, and neither cold nor hot, I will spue thee out of my mouth
17 Because thou sayest, I am rich, and increased with goods, and have need of nothing; and knowest not that thou art wretched, and miserable, and poor, and blind, and naked:
18 I counsel thee to buy of me gold tried in the fire, that thou mayest be rich; and white raiment, that thou mayest be clothed, and that the shame of thy nakedness do not appear; and anoint thine eyes with eyesalve, that thou mayest see
19 As many as I love, I rebuke and chasten: be zealous therefore, and repent

STRONGHOLD OF MISTRUST

IT IS WRITTEN:

Rev 12:11
11 And they overcame him by the blood of the Lamb, and by the word of their testimony; and they loved not their lives unto the death

2 Sam 22:3-4
3 The God of my rock; in him will I trust: he is my shield, and the horn of my salvation, my high tower, and my refuge, my saviour; thou savest me from violence
4 I will call on the LORD, who is worthy to be praised: so shall I be saved from mine enemies

2 Sam 22:31
31 As for God, his way is perfect; the word of the LORD is tried: he is a buckler to all them that trust in him

2 Sam 22:33
33 God is my strength and power: and he maketh my way perfect

1 Chr 5:20
20 And they were helped against them, and the Hagarites were delivered into their hand, and all that were with them: for they cried to God in the battle, and he was intreated of them; because they put their trust in him

Job 13:15
15 Though he slay me, yet will I trust in him: but I will maintain mine own

Ps 4:5
5 Offer the sacrifices of righteousness, and put your trust in the LORD

Ps 5:12
12 For thou, LORD, wilt bless the righteous; with favour wilt thou compass him as with a shield

Ps 7:1
1 O LORD my God, in thee do I put my trust: save me from all them that persecute me, and deliver me:

STRONGHOLD OF NEGATIVENESS

IT IS WRITTEN:

Rev 12:11
11 And they overcame him by the blood of the Lamb, and by the word of their testimony; and they loved not their lives unto the death

Ps 68:19
19 Blessed be the Lord, who daily loadeth us with benefits, even the God of our salvation Selah

Ps 68:32
32 Sing unto God, ye kingdoms of the earth; O sing praises unto the Lord; Selah:

Ps 70:2-4
2 Let them be ashamed and confounded that seek after my soul: let them be turned backward, and put to confusion, that desire my hurt
3 Let them be turned back for a reward of their shame that say, Aha, aha
4 Let all those that seek thee rejoice and be glad in thee: and let such as love thy salvation say continually, Let God be magnified

Ps 71:5-6
5 For thou art my hope, O Lord GOD: thou art my trust from my youth
6 By thee have I been holden up from the womb: thou art he that took me out of my mother's bowels: my praise shall be continually of thee

Ps 71:15-16
15 My mouth shall shew forth thy righteousness and thy salvation all the day; for I know not the numbers thereof
16 I will go in the strength of the Lord GOD: I will make mention of thy righteousness, even of thine only

Ps 72:17-19
17 His name shall endure forever: his name shall be continued as long as the sun: and men shall be blessed in him: all nations shall call him blessed
18 Blessed be the LORD God, the God of Israel, who only doeth wondrous things
19 And blessed be his glorious name for ever: and let the whole earth be filled with his glory; Amen, and Amen

STRONGHOLD OF OBESITY

IT IS WRITTEN:

Rev 12:11
11 And they overcame him by the blood of the Lamb, and by the word of their testimony; and they loved not their lives unto the death

Prov 23:1-3
1 When thou sittest to eat with a ruler, consider diligently what is before thee:
3 Be not desirous of his dainties: for they are deceitful meat

Prov 23:6
6 Eat thou not the bread of him that hath an evil eye, neither desire thou his dainty meats:

Prov 25:27-28
27 It is not good to eat much honey: so for men to search their own glory is not glory
28 He that hath no rule over his own spirit is like a city that is broken down, and without walls

Dan 1:12-16
12 Prove thy servants, I beseech thee, ten days; and let them give us pulse to eat, and water to drink
13 Then let our countenances be looked upon before thee, and the countenance of the children that eat of the portion of the king's meat: and as thou seest, deal with thy servants
14 So he consented to them in this matter, and proved them ten days
15 And at the end of ten days their countenances appeared fairer and fatter in flesh than all the children which did eat the portion of the king's meat
16 Thus Melzar took away the portion of their meat, and the wine that they should drink; and gave them pulse

Prov 30:8
8 Remove far from me vanity and lies: give me neither poverty nor riches; feed me with food convenient for me:

Job 23:12
12 Neither have I gone back from the commandment of his lips; I have esteemed the words of his mouth more than my necessary food

STRONGHOLD OF OPPRESSION

IT IS WRITTEN:

Rev 12:11
11 And they overcame him by the blood of the Lamb, and by the word of their testimony; and they loved not their lives unto the death

Deut 26:7-8
7 And when we cried unto the LORD God of our fathers, the LORD heard our voice, and looked on our affliction, and our labour, and our oppression:
8 And the LORD brought us forth out of Egypt with a mighty hand, and with an outstretched arm, and with great terribleness, and with signs, and with wonders:

Job 36:15
15 He delivereth the poor in his affliction, and openeth their ears in oppression

Ps 12:5
5 For the oppression of the poor, for the sighing of the needy, now will I arise, saith the LORD; I will set him in safety from him that puffeth at him

Ps 43:2-3
2 For thou art the God of my strength: why go I mourning because of the oppression of the enemy?
3 O send out thy light and thy truth: let them lead me; let them bring me unto thy holy hill, and to thy tabernacles

Ps 119:134-135
134 Deliver me from the oppression of man: so will I keep thy precepts
135 Make thy face to shine upon thy servant; and teach me thy statutes

Isa 54:14
14 In righteousness shalt thou be established: thou shalt be far from oppression; for thou shalt not fear: and from terror; for it shall not come near thee

Ezek 46:18
18 Moreover the prince shall not take of the people's inheritance by oppression, to thrust them out of their possession;

STRONGHOLD OF PAST HURTS

IT IS WRITTEN:

Rev 12:11
11 And they overcame him by the blood of the Lamb, and by the word of their testimony; and they loved not their lives unto the death

Rom 3:25
25 Whom God hath set forth to be a propitiation through faith in his blood, to declare his righteousness for the remission of sins that are past, through the forbearance of God;

Eph 2:2-6
2 Wherein in time past ye walked according to the course of this world, according to the prince of the power of the air, the spirit that now worketh in the children of disobedience:
3 Among whom also we all had our conversation in times past in the lusts of our flesh, fulfilling the desires of the flesh and of the mind; and were by nature the children of wrath, even as others
4 But God, who is rich in mercy, for his great love wherewith he loved us,
5 Even when we were dead in sins, hath quickened us together with Christ, (by grace ye are saved;)
6 And hath raised us up together, and made us sit together in heavenly places in Christ Jesus:

1 Pet 2:9-10
9 But ye are a chosen generation, a royal priesthood, an holy nation, a peculiar people; that ye should shew forth the praises of him who hath called you out of darkness into his marvellous light:
10 Which in time past were not a people, but are now the people of God: which had not obtained mercy, but now have obtained mercy

I Jn 2:8
8 Again, a new commandment I write unto you, which thing is true in him and in you: because the darkness is past, and the true light now shineth

Matt 6:15
15 But if ye forgive not men their trespasses, neither will your Father forgive your trespasses

STRONGHOLD OF POWER

IT IS WRITTEN:

Rev 12:11
11 And they overcame him by the blood of the Lamb, and by the word of their testimony; and they loved not their lives unto the death

Ps 66:7
7 He ruleth by his power for ever; his eyes behold the nations: let not the rebellious exalt themselves. Selah.

Ps 63:2-7
2 To see thy power and thy glory, so as I have seen thee in the sanctuary.
3 Because thy lovingkindness is better than life, my lips shall praise thee.
4 Thus will I bless thee while I live: I will lift up my hands in thy name.
5 My soul shall be satisfied as with marrow and fatness; and my mouth shall praise thee with joyful lips:
6 When I remember thee upon my bed, and meditate on thee in the night watches.
7 Because thou hast been my help, therefore in the shadow of thy wings will I rejoice.

Ps 62:11
11 God hath spoken once; twice have I heard this; that power belongeth unto God.

Ps 59:16-17
16 But I will sing of thy power; yea, I will sing aloud of thy mercy in the morning: for thou hast been my defence and refuge in the day of my trouble.
17 Unto thee, O my strength, will I sing: for God is my defence, and the God of my mercy.

Ps 106:8
8 Nevertheless he saved them for his name's sake, that he might make his mighty power to be known.

Ps 110:3
3 Thy people shall be willing in the day of thy power, in the beauties of holiness from the womb of the morning: thou hast the dew of thy youth.

STRONGHOLD OF POVERTY

IT IS WRITTEN:

Rev 12:11
11 And they overcame him by the blood of the Lamb, and by the word of their testimony; and they loved not their lives unto the death

Matt 6:33
33 But seek ye first the kingdom of God, and his righteousness; and all these things shall be added unto you

John 14:13
13 And whatsoever ye shall ask in my name, that will I do, that the Father may be glorified in the Son

Deut 29:9
9 Keep therefore the words of this covenant, and do them, that ye may prosper in all that ye do

Phil 4:19
19But my God shall supply all your need according to his riches in glory by Christ Jesus

Job 36:11
11 If they obey and serve him, they shall spend their days in prosperity, and their years in pleasures

Josh 1:8
8 This book of the law shall not depart out of thy mouth; but thou shalt meditate therein day and night, that thou mayest observe to do according to all that is written therein: for then thou shalt make thy way prosperous, and then thou shalt have good success

3 Jn 1:2
2 Beloved, I wish above all things that thou mayest prosper and be in health, even as thy soul prospereth

Gen 24:40
40 And he said unto me, The LORD, before whom I walk, will send his angel with thee, and prosper thy way;

STRONGHOLD OF PRIDE

IT IS WRITTEN:

Rev 12:11
11 And they overcame him by the blood of the Lamb, and by the word of their testimony; and they loved not their lives unto the death

Dan 5:20
20 But when his heart was lifted up, and his mind hardened in pride, he was deposed from his kingly throne, and they took his glory from him:

Prov 6:16-19
16 These six things doth the LORD hate: yea, seven are an abomination unto him:
17 A proud look, a lying tongue, and hands that shed innocent blood,
18 An heart that deviseth wicked imaginations, feet that be swift in running to mischief,
19 A false witness that speaketh lies, and he that soweth discord among brethren

Prov 16:18-19
18 Pride goeth before destruction, and an haughty spirit before a fall
19 Better it is to be of an humble spirit with the lowly, than to divide the spoil with the proud

I Jn 2:16-17
16 For all that is in the world, the lust of the flesh, and the lust of the eyes, and the pride of life, is not of the Father, but is of the world
17 And the world passeth away, and the lust thereof: but he that doeth the will of God abideth for ever

Ps 36:11
11 Let not the foot of pride come against me, and let not the hand of the wicked remove me

Ps 73:6
6 Therefore pride compasseth them about as a chain; violence covereth them as a garment

STRONGHOLD OF PROBLEMS

IT IS WRITTEN:

Rev 12:11
11 And they overcame him by the blood of the Lamb, and by the word of their testimony; and they loved not their lives unto the death

Ps 37:1-17
1 Fret not thyself because of evildoers, neither be thou envious against the workers of iniquity
2 For they shall soon be cut down like the grass, and wither as the green herb
3 Trust in the LORD, and do good; so shalt thou dwell in the land, and verily thou shalt be fed
4 Delight thyself also in the LORD; and he shall give thee the desires of thine heart
5 Commit thy way unto the LORD; trust also in him; and he shall bring it to pass
6 And he shall bring forth thy righteousness as the light, and thy judgment as the noonday
7 Rest in the LORD, and wait patiently for him: fret not thyself because of him who prospereth in his way, because of the man who bringeth wicked devices to pass
8 Cease from anger, and forsake wrath: fret not thyself in any wise to do evil
9 For evildoers shall be cut off: but those that wait upon the LORD, they shall inherit the earth
10 For yet a little while, and the wicked shall not be: yea, thou shalt diligently consider his place, and it shall not be
11 But the meek shall inherit the earth; and shall delight themselves in the abundance of peace
12 The wicked plotteth against the just, and gnasheth upon him with his teeth
13 The Lord shall laugh at him: for He seeth that his day is coming
14 The wicked have drawn out the sword, and have bent their bow, to cast down the poor and needy, and to slay such as be of upright conversation
15 Their sword shall enter into their own heart, and their bows shall be broken
16 A little that a righteous man hath is better than the riches of many wicked
17 the wicked shall be broken: but the LORD upholdeth the righteous

STRONGHOLD OF REBELLION

IT IS WRITTEN:

Rev 12:11
11 And they overcame him by the blood of the Lamb, and by the word of their testimony; and they loved not their lives unto the death

Exod 19:5
5 Now therefore, if ye will obey my voice indeed, and keep my covenant, then ye shall be a peculiar treasure unto me above all people: for all the earth is mine:

Jer 7:23
23 But this thing commanded I them, saying, Obey my voice, and I will be your God, and ye shall be my people: and walk ye in all the ways that I have commanded you, that it may be well unto you

Isa 1:19-20
19 If ye be willing and obedient, ye shall eat the good of the land:
20 But if ye refuse and rebel, ye shall be devoured with the sword: for the mouth of the LORD hath spoken it

Rom 6:16
16 Know ye not, that to whom ye yield yourselves servants to obey, his servants ye are to whom ye obey; whether of sin unto death, or of obedience unto righteousness?

2 Cor 10:5
5 Casting down imaginations, and every high thing that exalteth itself against the knowledge of God, and bringing into captivity every thought to the obedience of Christ;

1 Pet 1:13-14
13 Wherefore gird up the loins of your mind, be sober, and hope to the end for the grace that is to be brought unto you at the revelation of Jesus Christ;
14 As obedient children, not fashioning yourselves according to the former lusts in your ignorance:

Phil 2:5
5 Let this mind be in you, which was also in Christ Jesus:

STRONGHOLD OF REJECTION

IT IS WRITTEN:

Rev 12:11
11 And they overcame him by the blood of the Lamb, and by the word of their testimony; and they loved not their lives unto the death

Rom 5:19
19 For as by one man's disobedience many were made sinners, so by the obedience of one shall many be made righteous

James 5:16
16 The effectual fervent prayer of a righteous man availeth much

1 Pet 3:12
12 For the eyes of the Lord are over the righteous, and his ears are open unto their prayers:

2 Cor 5:17
17 Therefore if any man be in Christ, he is a new creature: old things are passed away; behold, all things are become new

Rom 8:10
10 And if Christ be in you, the body is dead because of sin; but the Spirit is life because of righteousness

Rom 10:4
4 For Christ is the end of the law for righteousness to everyone that believeth

2 Cor 5:21
21 For he hath made him to be sin for us, who knew no sin; that we might be made the righteousness of God in him

Ps 5:12
12 For thou, LORD, wilt bless the righteous; with favour wilt thou compass him as with a shield

Ps 32:11
12   Be glad in the LORD, and rejoice, ye righteous: and shout for joy, all ye that are upright in heart

STRONGHOLD OF RELIGION

IT IS WRITTEN:

Rev 12:11
11 And they overcame him by the blood of the Lamb, and by the word of their testimony; and they loved not their lives unto the death

Rom 15:7
7 Wherefore receive ye one another, as Christ also received us to the glory of God

Rom 13:10
10 Love worketh no ill to his neighbour: therefore love is the fulfilling of the law

John 15:12-13
12 This is my commandment, That ye love one another, as I have loved you
13 Greater love hath no man than this, that a man lay down his life for his friends

Rom 12:10
10 Be kindly affectioned one to another with brotherly love; in honour preferring one another;

Eph 4:32
32 And be ye kind one to another, tenderhearted, forgiving one another, even as God for Christ's sake hath forgiven you

Col 3:12-13
12 Put on therefore, as the elect of God, holy and beloved, bowels of mercies, kindness, humbleness of mind, meekness, longsuffering;
13 Forbearing one another, and forgiving one another, if any man have a quarrel against any: even as Christ forgave you, so also do ye

1Thes 3:12-13
12 And the Lord make you to increase and abound in love one toward another, and toward all men, even as we do toward you:
13 To the end he may stablish your hearts unblameable in holiness before God, even our Father, at the coming of our Lord Jesus Christ with all his saints

STRONGHOLD OF REVENGE

IT IS WRITTEN:

Rev 12:11
11 And they overcame him by the blood of the Lamb, and by the word of their testimony; and they loved not their lives unto the death

Rom 12:19-21
19 Dearly beloved, avenge not yourselves, but rather give place unto wrath: for it is written, Vengeance is mine; I will repay, saith the Lord
20 Therefore if thine enemy hunger, feed him; if he thirst, give him drink: for in so doing thou shalt heap coals of fire on his head
21 Be not overcome of evil, but overcome evil with good

Ps 149:5-9
5 Let the saints be joyful in glory: let them sing aloud upon their beds
6 Let the high praises of God be in their mouth, and a twoedged sword in their hand;
7 To execute vengeance upon the heathen, and punishments upon the people;
8 To bind their kings with chains, and their nobles with fetters of iron;
9 To execute upon them the judgment written: this honour have all his saints Praise ye the LORD

Isa 61:1-2
1 The Spirit of the Lord GOD is upon me; because the LORD hath anointed me to preach good tidings unto the meek; he hath sent me to bind up the brokenhearted, to proclaim liberty to the captives, and the opening of the prison to them that are bound;
2 To proclaim the acceptable year of the LORD, and the day of vengeance of our God; to comfort all that mourn;

Jer 51:36
36 Therefore thus saith the LORD; Behold, I will plead thy cause, and take vengeance for thee;

Nahum 1:2
2 God is jealous, and the LORD revengeth; the LORD revengeth, and is furious; the LORD will take vengeance on his adversaries, and he reserveth wrath for his enemies

STRONGHOLD OF SELFISHNESS

IT IS WRITTEN:

Rev 12:11
11 And they overcame him by the blood of the Lamb, and by the word of their testimony; and they loved not their lives unto the death

Prov 3:27-28
27 Withhold not good from them to whom it is due, when it is in the power of thine hand to do it
28 Say not unto thy neighbour, Go, and come again, and tomorrow I will give; when thou hast it by thee

Prov 25:21-22
21 If thine enemy be hungry, give him bread to eat; and if he be thirsty, give him water to drink:
22 For thou shalt heap coals of fire upon his head, and the LORD shall reward thee

Matt 5:42-44
42 Give to him that asketh thee, and from him that would borrow of thee turn not thou away
43 Ye have heard that it hath been said, Thou shalt love thy neighbour, and hate thine enemy
44 But I say unto you, Love your enemies, bless them that curse you, do good to them that hate you, and pray for them which despitefully use you, and persecute you;

Matt 10:8
8 Heal the sick, cleanse the lepers, raise the dead, cast out devils: freely ye have received, freely give

Matt 10:42
42 And whosoever shall give to drink unto one of these little ones a cup of cold water only in the name of a disciple, verily I say unto you, he shall in no wise lose his reward

Matt 14:16
16 But Jesus said unto them, They need not depart; give ye them to eat

STRONGHOLD OF SELF- PITY

IT IS WRITTEN:

Neh 2:2
2 Why is thy countenance sad, seeing thou art not sick? this is nothing else but sorrow of heart

Prov 15:13
13 A merry heart maketh a cheerful countenance: but by sorrow of the heart the spirit is broken

Eccl 11:10
10 Therefore remove sorrow from thy heart, and put away evil from thy flesh: for childhood and youth and vanity

Isa 14:3
3 And it shall come to pass in the day that the LORD shall give thee rest from thy sorrow, and from thy fear, and from the hard bondage wherein thou wast made to serve,

Isa 51:11
11 Therefore the redeemed of the LORD shall return, and come with singing unto Zion; and everlasting joy shall be upon their head: they shall obtain gladness and joy; and sorrow and mourning shall flee away

John 16:21
21 A woman when she is in travail hath sorrow, because her hour is come: but as soon as she is delivered of the child, she remembereth no more the anguish, for joy that a man is born into the world

Ps 145:8
8 The LORD is gracious, and full of compassion; slow to anger, and of great mercy

Isa 49:15
15 Can a woman forget her sucking child, that she should not have compassion on the son of her womb?

Matt 18:27
27 Then the lord of that servant was moved with compassion, and loosed him, and forgave him the debt

STRONGHOLD OF SHAME

IT IS WRITTEN:

Rev 12:11
11 And they overcame him by the blood of the Lamb, and by the word of their testimony; and they loved not their lives unto the death

Ps 35:4
4 Let them be confounded and put to shame that seek after my soul: let them be turned back and brought to confusion that devise my hurt

Ps 35:26
26 Let them be ashamed and brought to confusion together that rejoice at mine hurt: let them be clothed with shame and dishonour that magnify themselves against me

Ps 40:14
14 Let them be ashamed and confounded together that seek after my soul to destroy it; let them be driven backward and put to shame that wish me evil

Ps 44:7-8
7 But thou hast saved us from our enemies, and hast put them to shame that hated us
8 In God we boast all the day long, and praise thy name for ever Selah

Ps 71:24
24 My tongue also shall talk of thy righteousness all the day long: for they are confounded, for they are brought unto shame, that seek my hurt

Prov 3:35
35 The wise shall inherit glory: but shame shall be the promotion of fools

Isa 54:4
4 Fear not; for thou shalt not be ashamed: neither be thou confounded; for thou shalt not be put to shame: for thou shalt forget the shame of thy youth,

Ps 44:7-8
7 But thou hast saved us from our enemies, and hast put them to shame that hated us
8 In God we boast all the day long, and praise thy name for ever Selah

STRONGHOLD OF SICKNESS

IT IS WRITTEN:

Rev 12:11
11 And they overcame him by the blood of the Lamb, and by the word of their testimony; and they loved not their lives unto the death

Ps 107:20
20 He sent his word, and healed them, and delivered them from their destructions

Isa 53:5
5 But he was wounded for our transgressions, he was bruised for our iniquities: the chastisement of our peace was upon him; and with his stripes we are healed

Matt 4:24
24 And his fame went throughout all Syria: and they brought unto him all sick people that were taken with divers diseases and torments, and those which were possessed with devils, and those which were lunatick, and those that had the palsy; and he healed them

Matt 8:8
8 speak the word only, and my servant shall be healed

Matt 8:13
13 And Jesus said unto the centurion, Go thy way; and as thou hast believed, so be it done unto thee And his servant was healed in the selfsame hour

Matt 8:16
16 When the even was come, they brought unto him many that were possessed with devils: and he cast out the spirits with his word, and healed all that were sick:

1 Pet 2:24
24 Who his own self bare our sins in his own body on the tree, that we, being dead to sins, should live unto righteousness: by whose stripes ye were healed

STRONGHOLD OF SIN

IT IS WRITTEN:

Rev 12:11
11 And they overcame him by the blood of the Lamb, and by the word of their testimony; and they loved not their lives unto the death

Ps 32:1-2
1 Blessed is he whose transgression is forgiven, whose sin is covered
2 Blessed is the man unto whom the LORD imputeth not iniquity, and in whose spirit there is no guile

Ps 119:11
11 Thy word have I hid in mine heart, that I might not sin against thee

Eccl 5:6
6 Suffer not thy mouth to cause thy flesh to sin; neither say thou before the angel, that it was an error: wherefore should God be angry at thy voice, and destroy the work of thine hands?

Isa 6:7
7 And he laid it upon my mouth, and said, Lo, this hath touched thy lips; and thine iniquity is taken away, and thy sin purged

Isa 53:10
10 Yet it pleased the LORD to bruise him; he hath put him to grief: when thou shalt make his soul an offering for sin, he shall see his seed, he shall prolong his days, and the pleasure of the LORD shall prosper in his hand

Isa 53:12
12 Therefore will I divide him a portion with the great, and he shall divide the spoil with the strong; because he hath poured out his soul unto death: and he was numbered with the transgressors; and he bare the sin of many, and made intercession for the transgressors

Jer 31:34
Thus saith the LORD: for I will forgive their iniquity, and I will remember their sin no more

STRONGHOLD OF SORROW

IT IS WRITTEN:

Rev 12:11
11 And they overcame him by the blood of the Lamb, and by the word of their testimony; and they loved not their lives unto the death

Neh 8:10
10 Then he said unto them, Go your way, eat the fat, and drink the sweet, and send portions unto them for whom nothing is prepared: for this day is holy unto our Lord: neither be ye sorry; for the joy of the LORD is your strength

Job 33:26
26 He shall pray unto God, and he will be favourable unto him: and he shall see his face with joy: for he will render unto man his righteousness

Ps 5:11-12
11 But let all those that put their trust in thee rejoice: let them ever shout for joy, because thou defendest them: let them also that love thy name be joyful in thee
12 For thou, LORD, wilt bless the righteous; with favour wilt thou compass him as with a shield

Ps 16:11
11 Thou wilt shew me the path of life: in thy presence is fulness of joy; at thy right hand there are pleasures for evermore

Ps 27:6
6 And now shall mine head be lifted up above mine enemies round about me: therefore will I offer in his tabernacle sacrifices of joy; I will sing, yea, I will sing praises unto the LORD

Ps 33:1-5
1 Rejoice in the LORD, O ye righteous: for praise is comely for the upright
2 Praise the LORD with harp: sing unto him with the psaltery and an instrument of ten strings
3 Sing unto him a new song; play skillfully with a loud noise
4 For the word of the LORD is right; and all his works are done in truth
5 He loveth righteousness and judgment: the earth is full of the goodness of the LORD

STRONGHOLD OF THE SPIRIT OF HEAVINESS

IT IS WRITTEN:

Rev 12:11
11 And they overcame him by the blood of the Lamb, and by the word of their testimony; and they loved not their lives unto the death

1 Chr 16:35
35 And say ye, Save us, O God of our salvation, and gather us together, and deliver us from the heathen, that we may give thanks to thy holy name, and glory in thy praise

1 Chr 23:30
30 And to stand every morning to thank and praise the LORD, and likewise at even;

1 Chr 29:13
13 Now therefore, our God, we thank thee, and praise thy glorious name

Ps 9:1-10
1 I will praise thee, O LORD, with my whole heart; I will shew forth all thy marvelous works
2 I will be glad and rejoice in thee: I will sing praise to thy name, O thou most High
3 When mine enemies are turned back, they shall fall and perish at thy presence
4 For thou hast maintained my right and my cause; thou satest in the throne judging right
5 Thou hast rebuked the heathen, thou hast destroyed the wicked, thou hast put out their name for ever and ever
6 O thou enemy, destructions are come to a perpetual end: and thou hast destroyed cities; their memorial is perished with them
7 But the LORD shall endure forever: he hath prepared his throne for judgment
8And he shall judge the world in righteousness, he shall minister judgment to the people in uprightness
9 The LORD also will be a refuge for the oppressed, a refuge in times of trouble
10 And they that know thy name will put their trust in thee: for thou, LORD, hast not forsaken them that seek thee

STRONGHOLD OF STRESS

IT IS WRITTEN:

Rev 12:11
11 And they overcame him by the blood of the Lamb, and by the word of their testimony; and they loved not their lives unto the death

Ps 29:11
11The LORD will give strength unto his people; the LORD will bless his people with peace

Ps 55:18
18 He hath delivered my soul in peace from the battle that was against me: for there were many with me

Ps 85:10-13
10 Mercy and truth are met together; righteousness and peace have kissed each other
11 Truth shall spring out of the earth; and righteousness shall look down from heaven
12 Yea, the LORD shall give that which is good; and our land shall yield her increase
13 Righteousness shall go before him; and shall set us in the way of his steps

Prov 3:2-7
2 For length of days, and long life, and peace, shall they add to thee
3 Let not mercy and truth forsake thee: bind them about thy neck; write them upon the table of thine heart:
4 So shalt thou find favour and good understanding in the sight of God and man
5 Trust in the LORD with all thine heart; and lean not unto thine own understanding
6 In all thy ways acknowledge him, and he shall direct thy paths
7 Be not wise in thine own eyes: fear the LORD, and depart from evil

Isa 9:6
6 For unto us a child is born, unto us a son is given: and the government shall be upon his shoulder: and his name shall be called Wonderful, Counselor, The mighty God, The everlasting Father, The Prince of Peace

STRONGHOLD OF STRIFE

IT IS WRITTEN:

Rev 12:11
11 And they overcame him by the blood of the Lamb, and by the word of their testimony; and they loved not their lives unto the death

Gen 13:8
8 And Abram said unto Lot, Let there be no strife, I pray thee, between me and thee, and between my herdmen and thy herdmen; for we be brethren

Ps 31:20
20 Thou shalt hide them in the secret of thy presence from the pride of man: thou shalt keep them secretly in a pavilion from the strife of tongues

Prov 20:3
3 It is an honour for a man to cease from strife: but every fool will be

Rom 13:13-14
13 Let us walk honestly, as in the day; not in rioting and drunkenness, not in chambering and wantonness, not in strife and envying
14 But put ye on the Lord Jesus Christ, and make not provision for the flesh, to fulfill the lusts thereof

1 Cor 3:3-4
3 For ye are yet carnal: for whereas there is among you envying, and strife, and divisions, are ye not carnal, and walk as men?
4 For while one saith, I am of Paul; and another, I am of Apollos; are ye not carnal?

Phil 2:3
3 Let nothing be done through strife or vainglory; but in lowliness of mind let each esteem other better than themselves

James 3:16-18
16 For where envying and strife is, there is confusion and every evil work
17 But the wisdom that is from above is first pure, then peaceable, gentle, and easy to be intreated, full of mercy and good fruits, without partiality, and without hypocrisy
18 And the fruit of righteousness is sown in peace of them that make peac

STRONGHOLD OF TEMPTATION

IT IS WRITTEN:

Rev 12:11
11 And they overcame him by the blood of the Lamb, and by the word of their testimony; and they loved not their lives unto the death

Prov 25:28
28 He that hath no rule over his own spirit is like a city that is broken down, and without walls

Matt 6:10-13
10 Thy kingdom come Thy will be done in earth, as it is in heaven
11 Give us this day our daily bread
12 And forgive us our debts, as we forgive our debtors
13 And lead us not into temptation, but deliver us from evil: For thine is the kingdom, and the power, and the glory, forever Amen

Matt 26:41
41 Watch and pray, that ye enter not into temptation: the spirit indeed is willing, but the flesh is weak

1 Cor 10:13
13 There hath no temptation taken you but such as is common to man: but God is faithful, who will not suffer you to be tempted above that ye are able; but will with the temptation also make a way to escape, that ye may be able to bear it

James 1:13-17
13 Let no man say when he is tempted, I am tempted of God: for God cannot be tempted with evil, neither tempteth he any man:
14 But every man is tempted, when he is drawn away of his own lust, and enticed
15 Then when lust hath conceived, it bringeth forth sin: and sin, when it is finished, bringeth forth death
16 Do not err, my beloved brethren
17 Every good gift and every perfect gift is from above, and cometh down from the Father of lights

11 Behold, I come quickly: hold that fast which thou hast, that no man take thy crown

STRONGHOLD OF THIEVERY

IT IS WRITTEN:

Rev 12:11
11And they overcame him by the blood of the Lamb, and by the word of their testimony; and they loved not their lives unto the death

Lev 19:11
11 Ye shall not steal, neither deal falsely, neither lie one to another

Matt 19:18-19
18 He saith unto him, Which? Jesus said, Thou shalt do no murder, Thou shalt not commit adultery, Thou shalt not steal, Thou shalt not bear false witness,
19 Honour thy father and thy mother: and, Thou shalt love thy neighbor as thyself

Eph 4:28-30
28 Let him that stole steal no more: but rather let him labour, working with his hands the thing which is good, that he may have to give to him that needeth
29 Let no corrupt communication proceed out of your mouth, but that which is good to the use of edifying, that it may minister grace unto the hearers
30 And grieve not the holy Spirit of God, whereby ye are sealed unto the day of redemption

1 Pet 4:15-16
15 But let none of you suffer as a murderer, or as a thief, or as an evildoer, or as a busybody in other men's matters
16 Yet if any man suffer as a Christian, let him not be ashamed; but let him glorify God on this behalf

Matt 6:19
19 Lay not up for yourselves treasures upon earth, where moth and rust doth corrupt, and where thieves break through and steal:

Matt 6:20-21
20 But lay up for yourselves treasures in heaven, where neither moth nor rust doth corrupt, and where thieves do not break through nor steal:
21 For where your treasure is, there will your heart be also

STRONGHOLD OF THOUGHT

IT IS WRITTEN:

Rev 12:11
11 And they overcame him by the blood of the Lamb, and by the word of their testimony; and they loved not their lives unto the death

2 Cor 10:5
5 Casting down imaginations, and every high thing that exalteth itself against the knowledge of God, and bringing into captivity every thought to the obedience of Christ;

Rom 8:6
6 For to be carnally minded is death; but to be spiritually minded is life and peace

Phil 3:14-16
14 I press toward the mark for the prize of the high calling of God in Christ Jesus
15 Let us therefore, as many as be perfect, be thus minded: and if in any thing ye be otherwise minded, God shall reveal even this unto you
16 Nevertheless, whereto we have already attained, let us walk by the same rule, let us mind the same thing

Ps 40:5
5 Many, O LORD my God, are thy wonderful works which thou hast done, and thy thoughts which are to us-ward: they cannot be reckoned up in order unto thee: if I would declare and speak of them, they are more than can be numbered

Ps 94:19-23
19 In the multitude of my thoughts within me thy comforts delight my soul
20 Shall the throne of iniquity have fellowship with thee, which frameth mischief by a law?
21 They gather themselves together against the soul of the righteous, and condemn the innocent blood
22 But the LORD is my defence; and my God is the rock of my refuge
23 And he shall bring upon them their own iniquity, and shall cut them off in their own wickedness; yea, the LORD our God shall cut them off

STRONGHOLD OF TIMIDITY

IT IS WRITTEN:

Rev 12:11
11 And they overcame him by the blood of the Lamb, and by the word of their testimony; and they loved not their lives unto the death

Prov 28:1
1 but the righteous are bold as a lion

Eccl 8:4
4 Where the word of a king is, there is power:

Acts 4:13
13 Now when they saw the boldness of Peter and John, and perceived that they were unlearned and ignorant men, they marvelled; and they took knowledge of them, that they had been with Jesus

Acts 4:29-30
29 And now, Lord, behold their threatenings: and grant unto thy servants, that with all boldness they may speak thy word,
30 By stretching forth thine hand to heal; and that signs and wonders may be done by the name of thy holy child Jesus

Acts 4:31
31 And when they had prayed, the place was shaken where they were assembled together; and they were all filled with the Holy Ghost, and they spake the word of God with boldness

Eph 3:11-12
11 According to the eternal purpose which he purposed in Christ Jesus our Lord:
12 In whom we have boldness and access with confidence by the faith of him

Phil 1:20-21
20 According to my earnest expectation and my hope, that in nothing I shall be ashamed, but that with all boldness, as always, so now also Christ shall be magnified in my body, whether it be by life, or by death
21 For to me to live is Christ, and to die is gain

STRONGHOLD OF UNBELIEF

IT IS WRITTEN:

Rev 12:11
11 And they overcame him by the blood of the Lamb, and by the word of their testimony; and they loved not their lives unto the death

Matt 21:21
21 Jesus answered and said unto them, Verily I say unto you, If ye have faith, and doubt not, ye shall not only do this which is done to the fig tree, but also if ye shall say unto this mountain, Be thou removed, and be thou cast into the sea; it shall be done

Rom 12:3
3 For I say, through the grace given unto me, to every man that is among you, not to think of himself more highly than he ought to think; but to think soberly, according as God hath dealt to every man the measure of faith

Matt 17:20
20 If ye have faith as a grain of mustard seed, ye shall say unto this mountain, Remove hence to yonder place; and it shall remove; and nothing shall be impossible unto you

Mark 16:17-20
17 And these signs shall follow them that believe; In my name shall they cast out devils; they shall speak with new tongues;
18 They shall take up serpents; and if they drink any deadly thing, it shall not hurt them; they shall lay hands on the sick, and they shall recover
19 So then after the Lord had spoken unto them, he was received up into heaven, and sat on the right hand of God
20 And they went forth, and preached everywhere, the Lord working with them, and confirming the word with signs following Amen

Heb 4:11-12
11 Let us labour therefore to enter into that rest, lest any man fall after the same example of unbelief
12 For the word of God is quick, and powerful, and sharper than any two-edged sword, piercing even to the dividing asunder of soul and spirit, and of the joints and marrow, and is a discerner of the thoughts and intents of the heart

STRONGHOLD OF UNFORGIVENESS

IT IS WRITTEN:

Rev 12:11
11 And they overcame him by the blood of the Lamb, and by the word of their testimony; and they loved not their lives unto the death

Isa 55:7-9
7 Let the wicked forsake his way, and the unrighteous man his thoughts: and let him return unto the LORD, and he will have mercy upon him; and to our God, for he will abundantly pardon
8 For my thoughts are not your thoughts, neither are your ways my ways, saith the LORD
9 For as the heavens are higher than the earth, so are my ways higher than your ways, and my thoughts than your thoughts

Gen 50:17
17 Forgive, I pray thee now, the trespass of thy brethren, and their sin; for they did unto thee evil: and now, we pray thee, forgive the trespass of the servants of the God of thy father And Joseph wept when they spake unto him

2 Chr 7:14
14 If my people, which are called by my name, shall humble themselves, and pray, and seek my face, and turn from their wicked ways; then will I hear from heaven, and will forgive their sin, and will heal their land

Matt 6:12
12 And forgive us our debts, as we forgive our debtors

Matt 6:14-15
14 For if ye forgive men their trespasses, your heavenly Father will also forgive you:
15 But if ye forgive not men their trespasses, neither will your Father forgive your trespasses

Matt 18:21-22
21 Then came Peter to him, and said, Lord, how oft shall my brother sin against me, and I forgive him? till seven times?
22 Jesus saith unto him, I say not unto thee, Until seven times: but, Until seventy times seven

STRONGHOLD OF UNRIGHTEOUSNESS

IT IS WRITTEN:

Rev 12:11
11 And they overcame him by the blood of the Lamb, and by the word of their testimony; and they loved not their lives unto the death

Deut 25:1
1 If there be a controversy between men, and they come unto judgment, that the judges may judge them; then they shall justify the righteous, and condemn the wicked

IKing 8:32
32 Then hear thou in heaven, and do, and judge thy servants, condemning the wicked, to bring his way upon his head; and justifying the righteous, to give him according to his righteousness

II Ki 10:9
9 And it came to pass in the morning, that he went out, and stood, and said to all the people, Ye be righteous:

2 Chr 12:6
6 Whereupon the princes of Israel and the king humbled themselves; and they said, The LORD is righteous

Job 17:9
9 The righteous also shall hold on his way, and he that hath clean hands shall be stronger and stronger

Ps 1:6
6 For the LORD knoweth the way of the righteous: but the way of the ungodly shall perish

Rom 5:19
19 For as by one man's disobedience many were made sinners, so by the obedience of one shall many be made righteous

2 Tim 4:8
8 Henceforth there is laid up for me a crown of righteousness, which the Lord, the righteous judge, shall give me at that day: and not to me only, but unto all them also that love his appearing

STRONGHOLD OF VIOLENCE

IT IS WRITTEN:

Rev 12:11
11 And they overcame him by the blood of the Lamb, and by the word of their testimony; and they loved not their lives unto the death

Exod 14:14
14 The LORD shall fight for you, and ye shall hold your peace

Lev 26:6
6 And I will give peace in the land, and ye shall lie down, and none shall make you afraid: and I will rid evil beasts out of the land, neither shall the sword go through your land

Exod 14:14
14 The LORD shall fight for you, and ye shall hold your peace

Lev 26:6
6 And I will give peace in the land, and ye shall lie down, and none shall make you afraid: and I will rid evil beasts out of the land, neither shall the sword go through your land

Ps 29:11
11The LORD will give strength unto his people; the LORD will bless his people with peace

Ps 37:11
11 But the meek shall inherit the earth; and shall delight themselves in the abundance of peace

Ps 37:37
37 Mark the perfect man, and behold the upright: for the end of that man is peace

Ps 55:18
18 He hath delivered my soul in peace from the battle that was against me: for there were many with me

Prov 3:1-2
1 My son, forget not my law; but let thine heart keep my commandments:

STRONGHOLD OF WEAKNESS

IT IS WRITTEN:

Rev 12:11
11 And they overcame him by the blood of the Lamb, and by the word of their testimony; and they loved not their lives unto the death

Exod 15:2
2 The LORD is my strength and song, and he is become my salvation: he is my God, and I will prepare him an habitation; my father's God, and I will exalt him

Exod 15:3
3 The LORD is a man of war: the LORD is his name

Deut 33:25
25 Thy shoes shall be iron and brass; and as thy days, so shall thy strength be

1 Sam 2:10
10 The adversaries of the LORD shall be broken to pieces; out of heaven shall he thunder upon them: the LORD shall judge the ends of the earth; and he shall give strength unto his king, and exalt the horn of his anointed

2 Sam 22:33
33 God is my strength and power: and he maketh my way perfect

2 Sam 22:40
40 For thou hast girded me with strength to battle: them that rose up against me hast thou subdued under me

1 Chr 16:11-12
11 Seek the LORD and his strength, seek his face continually
12 Remember his marvellous works that he hath done, his wonders, and the judgments of his mouth;

Ps 18:2
2 The LORD is my rock, and my fortress, and my deliverer; my God, my strength, in whom I will trust; my buckler, and the horn of my salvation, and my high tower

STRONGHOLD OF WORRY

IT IS WRITTEN:

Rev 12:11
11 And they overcame him by the blood of the Lamb, and by the word of their testimony; and they loved not their lives unto the death

Josh 1:8
8 This book of the law shall not depart out of thy mouth; but thou shalt meditate therein day and night, that thou mayest observe to do according to all that is written therein: for then thou shalt make thy way prosperous, and then thou shalt have good success

Ps 1:2
2 But his delight is in the law of the LORD; and in his law doth he meditate day and night

Ps 63:6-7
6 When I remember thee upon my bed, and meditate on thee in the night watches
7 Because thou hast been my help, therefore in the shadow of thy wings will I rejoice

Ps 77:11-12
11 I will remember the works of the LORD: surely I will remember thy wonders of old
12 I will meditate also of all thy work, and talk of thy doings

Ps 119:14-16
14 I have rejoiced in the way of thy testimonies, as much as in all riches
15 I will meditate in thy precepts, and have respect unto thy ways
16 I will delight myself in thy statutes: I will not forget thy word

Ps 119:47-48
47 And I will delight myself in thy commandments, which I have loved
48 My hands also will I lift up unto thy commandments, which I have loved; and I will meditate in thy statutes

Prov 3:5-6
4   Trust in the LORD with all thine heart; and lean not unto thine own understanding

1 Cor 2:9-3:1

9 But as it is written, Eye hath not seen, nor ear heard, neither have entered into the heart of man, the things which God hath prepared for them that love him.

10 But God hath revealed them unto us by his Spirit: for the Spirit searcheth all things, yea, the deep things of God.

11 For what man knoweth the things of a man, save the spirit of man which is in him? even so the things of God knoweth no man, but the Spirit of God.

12 Now we have received, not the spirit of the world, but the spirit which is of God; that we might know the things that are freely given to us of God.

13 Which things also we speak, not in the words which man's wisdom teacheth, but which the Holy Ghost teacheth; comparing spiritual things with spiritual.

14 But the natural man receiveth not the things of the Spirit of God: for they are foolishness unto him: neither can he know them, because they are spiritually discerned.

15 But he that is spiritual judgeth all things, yet he himself is judged of no man.

16 For who hath known the mind of the Lord, that he may instruct him? But we have the mind of Christ.

BLESSINGS,

WATCHMEN RON AND CAROL

HAIMAHOUSE MINISTRIES, INC.

19513448R00097

Made in the USA
Charleston, SC
28 May 2013